Introduction

Welcome to *The Bells! The Bells!* It has been a joy to put together this compilation of quotes, stories, jokes and anecdotes about marriage.

I won't hide it from you… I am a big fan of marriage. I have been married to my wife Alie for twenty-five years. We have had some challenging times, yes, but then, a smooth sea never made a skilful mariner. It's the storms that refine and define you as a couple. Get through them together, and you have a shared treasure-chest of experiences that says to the world, 'We've pushed through and won, and won as a team!' I wouldn't swap that for anything. You come out the other side of every trial a much wiser person if you want to.

As the saying goes, 'Suffering can make you bitter or it can make you better. One letter makes the difference, the letter "I". I make the difference!' It's always a choice, but then love is a choice.

Alie and I were married in 1983 after a very romantic engagement. We fell in love at Cambridge University where Alie was studying Natural Sciences and I was studying (in a much looser sense) English Literature. I will never forget the exhilarating feeling of walking arm in arm through the streets of Cambridge during the Christmas of 1981, the snow falling all around us. I remember the first kiss… Wow! And the first movie we went to – *Arthur*, starring Dudley Moore and Liza Minnelli. The song of the movie by Christopher Cross ('Once in your Life You Find Her') became our song too.

I remember getting engaged and then preparing for the wedding service at Southwell Minister on 30 July 1983. The day itself was glorious: bright sunshine, beautiful bridesmaids (especially my twin sister), great music and a very eccentric photographer. I remember driving away from the service in our £300 Austin Healey Sprite (an uncovered, two-seater sports car dating from 1968). Most of the guests thought it was a joke. But it wasn't. It was our car, and it was all we could afford. We were penniless but we were happy.

And then, of course, romance began to turn to reality. We had to face the challenge of starting our married life with very little money. Then there was our first child – our lovely son Philip, who cried and cried and cried (he had colic), and the great trial of post-natal depression, an extended dark night of the soul that Alie got through, but only just. There was my job too – a first posting in Nottingham which stretched me to breaking-point. Somehow we endured the trials and made it to the next season, a season of more learning

– three more children, a cat and a black Labrador helped the educational process.

Today, as we prepare for our twenty-fifth wedding anniversary, I can safely say that my wife Alie is my best friend, my most loyal supporter, my most reliable critic, and my most valued confidante. I can't begin to imagine life without her. The occasional thought of that possibility brings my world crashing down around me, like imploding towers.

One thing both Alie and I would say is this. We are still together and indeed thriving (as opposed to surviving) because of our shared faith in God. When we made our promises before God in Southwell Minster twenty-five years ago, we really believed then (as we do now) that those promises were made to one who is alive – namely, Jesus – who rose from the dead and lives forever. Both Alie and I had been Christians already for a number of years and I was on my way to becoming an ordained priest in the Church of England. Our Christian faith meant everything to us then and means everything to us now.

I have taken hundreds and hundreds of weddings over the years. One of my favourite Bible readings for a wedding service is Ecclesiastes 4:9–12:

> *Two are better than one,*
> *because they have a good return for their work:*
> *If one falls down,*
> *his friend can help him up.*
> *But pity the man who falls*
> *and has no one to help him up!*
> *Also, if two lie down together, they will keep warm.*
> *But how can one keep warm alone?*
> *Though one may be overpowered,*
> *two can defend themselves.*
> *A cord of three strands is not quickly broken.*

That last sentence says it all for me. A cord of three strands is very difficult to tear. In our marriage, there have always been three people – Alie, me and God. God is the third person who has strengthened our resolve, tightened up our values, intensified our passion and empowered us with his Spirit. He is the one who has helped us to forgive each other on the many occasions when that has been necessary. He is the one who has enabled us to get through the good and the bad days. He is the one who has excited us with vision and with hope.

MONARCH
BOOKS

Oxford, UK, & Grand Rapids, Michigan, USA

First published in the UK in 2009 by Monarch Books
(a publishing imprint of Lion Hudson plc),
Wilkinson House, Jordan Hill Road, Oxford OX2 8DR.
Tel: +44 (0)1865 302750 Fax: +44 (0)1865 302757
Email: monarch@lionhudson.com
www.lionhudson.com

ISBN: 978-1-85424-893-0 (UK)
ISBN: 978-0-8254-6297-9 (USA)

Distributed by:
UK: Marston Book Services Ltd, PO Box 269, Abingdon, Oxon OX14 4YN;
USA: Kregel Publications, PO Box 2607, Grand Rapids, Michigan 49501

This book has been printed on
paper and board independently certified as
having come from sustainable forests.

British Library Cataloguing Data
A catalogue record for this book is available from
the British Library.

Printed and bound in Malta by Gutenberg Press.

First published in the UK in 2009 by Monarch Books
(a publishing imprint of Lion Hudson plc),
Wilkinson House, Jordan Hill Road, Oxford OX2 8DR.
Tel: +44 (0)1865 302750 Fax: +44 (0)1865 302757
Email: monarch@lionhudson.com
www.lionhudson.com

ISBN: 978-1-85424-893-0 (UK)
ISBN: 978-0-8254-6297-9 (USA)

Distributed by:
UK: Marston Book Services Ltd, PO Box 269, Abingdon, Oxon OX14 4YN;
USA: Kregel Publications, PO Box 2607, Grand Rapids, Michigan 49501

This book has been printed on
paper and board independently certified as
having come from sustainable forests.

British Library Cataloguing Data
A catalogue record for this book is available from
the British Library.

Printed and bound in Malta by Gutenberg Press.

The Bells! The Bells!

A Collection of the Finest Stories,

Jokes, Quotes and Readings about Marriage,

Beauty and Romance

Compiled by

Mark Stibbe

MONARCH
BOOKS

Oxford, UK, & Grand Rapids, Michigan, USA

Acknowledgements

Our thanks to those who have given us permission to use material reproduced in this collection. Every effort has been made to trace the original copyright holders where required. In some cases this has proved impossible. We shall be happy to correct any such omissions in future editions.

Note to church magazine editors

Today, Alie and I often say, 'Where would be without Jesus?' I remember one argument that was off the Richter scale. We were walking with our black Labrador Mij on a beach in North Norfolk. We were steaming with anger and decided we had had enough. We walked away from each other until Alie was a silhouette on the horizon.

Suddenly both of us became aware of our dog. We turned towards each other to find Mij exactly equidistant between us, turning to Alie, then to me, in frenetic and desperate movements, not knowing who to follow. Suddenly the silliness of what we were doing overwhelmed both of us and we both started walking towards each other, until husband, wife and exuberant dog were reconciled. I believe that God used our dog that day to tighten up the three-stranded cord of love.

I don't know everything about marriage – far from it. I have merely – to alter a Newtonian phrase – cleaned a few pebbles before the vast sea of marital wisdom. But twenty-five years of marriage, plus the same number of years preparing people for marriage, conducting weddings and advising married couples (as well as, inevitably, helping those whose marriages have broken up), has taught me something.

"Can we go home now, I've worked my tail off, my paws hurt, my head's spinning and there are no lamp posts in sight!"

Perhaps, more than anything, it has taught me that marriage is supposed to be like Andrex toilet paper – soft, strong and very long (and ideally, accompanied by at least one Labrador puppy). That is what it is meant to be. And when it is, it is brilliant!

I hope and pray that you enjoy this selection of the best material I have found and used at countless wedding services and receptions over nearly three decades. If you are preparing for your own wedding, my prayer is that God will use the treasure in this book to excite and to envision you. Too many couples are so fixated on getting ready for their wedding that they fail to get ready for their marriage. I pray that this book will help you to embrace the great adventure of marriage with your eyes wide open and not (like Tom Cruise and Nicole Kidman in their movie) with eyes wide shut.

These are difficult times for the sacred covenant of marriage. May this book be used to restore confidence in the highest form of relationship that human beings can aspire to.

God bless you, wherever you are on the epic and lifelong journey of matrimony.

Mark Stibbe
May 2008

Acceptance

ACCEPT: the secret of a good marriage

- Attraction
- Communication
- Commitment
- Enjoyment
- Purpose
- Trust

Anon

Age

The question is asked, 'Is there anything more beautiful in life than a young couple clasping hands and pure hearts in the path of marriage? Can there be anything more beautiful than young love?'

And the answer is given: 'Yes, there is a more beautiful thing. It is the spectacle of an old man and an old woman finishing their journey together on that path. Their hands are gnarled, but still clasped; their faces are seamed, but still radiant; their hearts are physically bowed and tired, but still strong with love and devotion for one another. Yes, there is a more beautiful thing than young love. Old love.'

Anon

The Three Ages of Man

When you have the time and the energy, you don't have the money.
When you have the money and the energy, you don't have the time.
When you have the money and the time, you don't have the energy.

Grandma and Grandpa were sitting outside watching the beautiful sunset and reminiscing about 'the good old days,' when Grandma turned to Grandpa and said, 'Darling, do you remember when we first started dating and you used to just casually reach over and take my hand?'

Grandpa looked over at her, smiled and took her aged hand in his.

With a wry little smile Grandma pressed a little further: 'Darling, do you remember how after we were engaged you'd sometimes lean over and suddenly kiss me on the cheek?'

Grandpa leaned slowly toward Grandma and gave her a lingering kiss on her wrinkled cheek.

Growing bolder still, Grandma said, 'Darling, do you remember how, after we were first married, you'd kind of nibble on my ear?'

Grandpa slowly got up from his rocker and headed into the house.

Alarmed, Grandma said, 'Darling, where are you going?'

Grandpa replied, 'To get my teeth!'

*We do not stop playing because we grow old;
we grow old because we stop playing.*

Anon

A little old couple walked slowly into McDonald's one cold winter evening. They looked out of place amid the young families and young couples eating there that night.

Some of the customers looked admiringly at them. You could tell what the admirers were thinking. 'Look, there is a couple who have been through a lot together, probably for sixty years or more!'

The little old man walked right up to the cash register, placed his order with no hesitation and then paid for their meal. The couple took a table near the back wall and started taking food off the tray. There was one hamburger, one order of French fries and one drink.

The little old man unwrapped the plain hamburger and carefully cut it in half. He placed one half in front of his wife. Then he carefully counted out the French fries, divided them into two piles and neatly placed one pile in front of his wife.

He took a sip of the drink, his wife took a sip and then set the cup down between them.

As the man began to eat his few bites of hamburger, the crowd began to get restless. Again you could tell what they were thinking. 'That poor old couple. All they can afford is one meal for the two of them.'

As the man began to eat his French fries one young man stood and came over to the old couple's table. He politely offered to buy another meal for them to eat. The old man replied that they were just fine. They were used to sharing everything.

Then the crowd noticed that the little old lady hadn't eaten a bite. She just sat there watching her husband eat and occasionally taking turns sipping the drink. Again the young man came over and begged them to let him buy them something to eat. This time the lady explained that no, they were used to sharing everything together.

As the little old man finished eating and was wiping his face neatly with a napkin, the young man could stand it no longer. Again he came over to their table and offered to buy some food. After being politely refused again, he finally asked a question of the little old lady.

'Ma'am, why aren't you eating? You said that you share everything. What is it that you are waiting for?'

She answered, 'The teeth.'

Jacob, age 92, and Rebecca, age 89, are all excited about their decision to get married. They go for a stroll to discuss the wedding and on the way they pass a chemist. Jacob suggests they go in.

He addresses the man behind the counter: 'Are you the owner?'

The pharmacist answers 'Yes.'

Says Jacob: 'We're about to get married. Do you sell heart medication?'

Pharmacist: 'Of course we do.'

Jacob: 'How about medicine for circulation?'

Pharmacist: 'All kinds.'

Jacob: 'Medicine for rheumatism, scoliosis?'

Pharmacist: 'Definitely.'

Jacob: 'How about Viagra?'

Pharmacist: 'Of course.'

Jacob: 'Medicine for memory problems, arthritis, jaundice?'

Pharmacist: 'Yes, a large variety. The works.'

Jacob: 'What about vitamins, sleeping pills, Geritol, antidotes for Parkinson's disease?'

Pharmacist: 'Absolutely.'

Jacob: 'You sell wheelchairs and walkers?'

Pharmacist: 'All speeds and sizes.'

Jacob says to the pharmacist: 'We'd like to register here for our wedding gifts, please.'

Grow old along with me.
The best is yet to be – the last of life for which the first was made.

Robert Browning

A wedding anniversary is the celebration of love, trust, partnership, tolerance and tenacity. The order varies for any given year.

Paul Sweeney

THE TOP TEN THINGS NOT TO SAY ON YOUR ANNIVERSARY

10. I stopped caring about anniversaries when you stopped caring about cooking.
9. Today is our what?
8. Okay, let's celebrate, but do we have to celebrate together?
7. I thought we only celebrated important events.
6. You can celebrate anniversaries with your next husband.
5. You don't like what I pick out, so I thought why bother?
4. I got you a present worth a pound for every time you were nice to me this year. Here's a £5 gift voucher for McDonald's.
3. If you want me to pretend that I care about our anniversary, I will.
2. You want to go out to dinner? Okay, okay, I'll take you to Pizza Hut if it'll shut ya up.
1. I thought you only had to celebrate anniversaries while you were still in love.

While enjoying an early morning breakfast in a northern Arizona cafe, four elderly ranchers were discussing everything from cattle, horses and weather, to how things used to be in the 'good old days'. Eventually the conversation moved on to their spouses.

One gentleman turned to the fellow on his right and asked, 'Roy, aren't you and your bride celebrating your fiftieth wedding anniversary soon?'

'Yup, we sure are,' Roy replied.

'Well, are you gonna do anything special to celebrate?' another man asked.

The old gentleman pondered this for a moment, then replied, 'For our twenty-fifth anniversary, I took Bea to Tucson. Maybe for our fiftieth, I'll go down there and get her.'

"Honey, how sweet of you to come all this way to help us celebrate our 25th!"

Our wedding was many years ago. The celebration continues to this day.

Gene Perret

Appreciation

*B*ob attended a seminar on interpersonal relationships and became convinced that he needed to do a better job of showing appreciation to his wife. So on his way home from work he picked up a dozen long-stem roses and a box of chocolates. He was eager to see how excited his wife would be at this example of appreciation.

As Bob walked in the door with a big grin, he met his wife in the hallway – and she burst into tears.

'What's wrong, honey?' Bob asked.

'It's been a terrible day!' she exclaimed. 'First, Tommy tried to flush a nappy down the toilet. Then the dishwasher stopped working. Sally came home from school with her legs all scratched, and now you come home drunk!'

In one of his famous Lake Woebegon monologues, humorist Garrison Keillor described a long-married couple. Every night the husband consumed a generous portion of the same menu offering. (Breaded veal cutlets, as I recall.) Every night over the course of four decades, the husband devoured the cutlets, wiped his face with a napkin, pushed his chair away from the table and looked his wife in the eye. He smiled at her and spoke in a tender voice: 'That's the best you've ever done.' It may sound monotonous to you, but to her his words of appreciation sounded like sweet music.

Norm Bales

Jill tells her husband, 'Jack, that young couple who just moved in next door seem such a loving twosome. Every morning, when he leaves the house, he kisses her goodbye, and every evening when he comes homes, he brings her a dozen roses. Now, why can't you do that?'

'Gosh,' Jack says, 'but I hardly know the girl!'

Assertiveness

A *man went on an assertiveness course at work, and as a result he decided that things needed to change at home, too.*

When he got home he told his wife: 'I want supper on the table each evening when I get home from work. I want you to run me a hot bath and scrub my back. Then I want you to turn back the sheets, warm the bed and lay out my pyjamas. And in the morning, do you know who's going to button my shirt and tie my tie?'

'Yes,' replied his wife. 'The undertaker.'

A man and a woman, who have never met before, find themselves assigned to the same sleeping-room on a transcontinental train.

Although initially embarrassed and uneasy over sharing a room, the two are tired and fall asleep quickly – he in the upper bunk and she in the lower.

At 2 a.m., he leans over and gently wakes the woman, saying, 'Ma'am, I'm sorry to bother you, but would you be willing to reach into the closet to get me a second blanket? I'm awfully cold.'

'I have a better idea,' she replies. 'Just for tonight, let's pretend that we're married.'

'Wow! That's a great idea!' he exclaims.

'Good,' she replies. 'Get your own blanket.'

Wife, just coming home to husband:
'I've been to karate class, so dinner will be late. Want to make something of it?'

Baldness

I love bald men. Just because you've lost your fuzz, don't mean you ain't a peach.

Dolly Parton

The big advantage of being bald is that you can style your hair with a damp cloth!

Grey hair is a blessing – ask any bald man.

God made just so many perfect heads; the rest he covered with hair.

Real men don't waste their hormones growing hair.

God is good, God is fair; To some he gave brains, to others hair!

This is not a bald spot – it's a solar panel for brain power!

Beauty

Soon after our last child left home for college, my husband was resting next to me on the couch with his head in my lap. I carefully removed his glasses.

'You know, honey,' I said sweetly, 'without your glasses you look like the same handsome young man I married.'

'Honey,' he replied with a grin, 'without my glasses, you still look pretty good too!'

Valerie L. Runyan

A husband and wife are shopping in their local Tesco and the husband picks up a crate of Stella and puts it in their trolley.

'What do you think you're doing?' asks his wife.

'They're on offer – only a tenner for twelve cans!' he replies.

'Put them back – we can't afford them!' declares his wife, and so they carry on shopping.

A few aisles further along, the woman picks up a £20 jar of facecream and puts it in the trolley.

'What do you think you're doing?' asks the husband.

'It's my facecream. It makes me look beautiful,' replies his wife.

Her husband retorts: 'So does twelve cans of Stella, and it's half the price!'

A man said to his wife one day, 'I don't know how you can be so stupid and so beautiful all at the same time.'

The wife responded, 'Allow me to explain it to you. God made me beautiful so you would be attracted to me. God made me stupid so I would be attracted to you!'

I'm tired of all this nonsense about beauty being only skin deep. That's deep enough! What do you want? An adorable pancreas?

Jean Kerr

You can take no credit for beauty at sixteen. But if you are beautiful at sixty, it will be your soul's own doing.

Marie Stopes

Anyone who keeps the ability to see beauty never grows old.

Franz Kafka

Benefits

Marriage is a career which brings about more benefits than many others.

Simone de Beauvoir

Both men and women live longer, happier, healthier and wealthier lives when they are married. Unmarried cohabitation doesn't cut it. Cohabitation does not bring the benefits – in physical health, wealth, and emotional wellbeing – that marriage does. And, married people have both more and better sex than do their unmarried counterparts.

Linda Waite

Bible

A man and his wife were having an argument about who should brew the coffee each morning.

The wife said, 'You should do it because you get up first, and then we don't have to wait as long to get our coffee.'

The husband said, 'You are in charge of cooking around here and you should do it, because that is your job, and I can just wait for my coffee.'

The wife replied, 'No, you should do it, and besides, it says in the Bible that the man should do the coffee.'

The husband replied, 'I can't believe that – show me!'

So she fetched the Bible, and opened the New Testament and showed him that at the top of several pages, it indeed says, 'Hebrews.'

Have you ever wondered if the Bible has any tips on how to find the girl of your dreams? Good news! There are numerous biblical examples for you to consider:

- Find an attractive prisoner of war, bring her home, shave her head, trim her nails, and give her new clothes – then she's yours (Deuteronomy 21:11–13).
- Find a prostitute and marry her (Hosea 1:1–3).
- Find a man with seven daughters and impress him by watering his flock (Moses – Exodus 2:16–21).
- Purchase a piece of property and get a woman as part of the deal (Boaz – Ruth 4:5–10).
- Go to a party and hide. When the women come out to dance, grab one and carry her off to be your wife (Judges 21:19–25).
- Have God create a wife for you while you sleep. But be careful; it'll cost you a rib (Adam – Genesis 2:19–24).
- Agree to work seven years in exchange for a woman's hand in marriage. Get tricked into marrying the wrong woman, then work another seven years for the woman you wanted to marry in the first place. That's right. Fourteen years of hard labour for a wife (Jacob – Genesis 29:15–30).
- Cut 200 foreskins off the enemies of your future father-in-law and get his daughter in exchange (David – 1 Samuel 18:27).
- Even if no one is out there, just wander around a bit and you'll find someone. Maybe your sister (Cain – Genesis 4:16–17).
- Become the emperor of a huge nation and hold a beauty contest (Xerxes – Esther 2:3–4).
- When you see someone you like, go home and tell your parents, 'I have seen a woman I like. Now get her for me.' If your parents question your decision, simply say, 'Get her for me. She's the one for me' (Samson – Judges 14:1–3).
- Kill any husband and take his wife (David – 2 Samuel 11).
- Wait for your brother to die, then take his widow. It's not just a good idea; it's the law (Deuteronomy and Leviticus; see Boaz in the book of Ruth).

*"It's a complete package, my lord. With additional 28 days
cooling off period and full camel-back guarantee."*

Blessings

May you never forget what is worth remembering or remember what is best forgotten.

May your joys be as deep as the ocean, and your troubles as light as its foam.

May the road rise to meet you.
May the wind be always at your back.
May the sun shine warm upon your face,
The rains fall soft upon the fields.

May the light of friendship guide your paths together.
May the laughter of children grace the halls of your home.
May the joy of living for one another trip a smile from your lips,
A twinkle from your eye.

And when eternity beckons,
at the end of a life heaped high with love,
May the good Lord embrace you
with the arms that have nurtured you
the whole length of your joy-filled days.
May the gracious God hold you both
in the palm of His hands.

And, today, may the Spirit of Love
find a dwelling place in your hearts.
Amen.

An Irish wedding blessing

Beatitudes for a married couple

Blessed are the husband and wife who continue to be affectionate, considerate and loving after the wedding bells have stopped ringing.

Blessed are the husband and wife who are as polite and courteous to one another as they are to their friends.

Blessed are they who have a sense of humour; their marriage shall be much brighter.

Blessed are they who are faithful to each other and mutually helpful. God will surely guide them.

Blessed are the husband and wife who thank God for good things which come to them. They shall receive both good things and thankful children.

Blessed are the parents who recognize their children as gifts from God; their home shall be filled with love.

Blessed are those mates who make their home a place 'where seldom is heard a discouraging word'. They shall inspire others to do likewise.

Blessed are the parents who attend and support their church. Their children shall develop a strong faith.

Blessed is the couple who are good stewards of all God's gifts; their children will bless them and follow their example.

Blessed are all those whose lives are a testimony of faith in God; they shall be the channels through which God's kingdom will come on earth.

Surely goodness and mercy shall follow them all the days of their lives and they shall dwell in the house of the Lord forever.

Cars

When a man opens a car door for his wife, it's either a new car or a new wife.

Prince Philip

The 'car way' of telling what stage a relationship is at:

- *Trying to impress the woman:* The man unlocks and opens the door, waits for her to get inside, then closes her door behind her.
- *Dating:* He unlocks her door and then goes around to his side to get in.
- *Engaged:* He opens his door, leans over and unlocks her door and opens it.
- *Married:* He gets into the driver's seat, unlocks her door, and says, 'Aren't you getting in?'

WIFE:	'There's trouble with the car. It has water in the carburettor.'
HUSBAND:	'Water in the carburettor? That's ridiculous.'
WIFE:	'I tell you, the car has water in the carburettor!'
HUSBAND:	'You don't even know what a carburettor is. Where's the car?'
WIFE:	'In the swimming pool.'

Cats

A man hated his wife's cat and one day decided to get rid of it. He drove twenty blocks away from home and dropped the cat there. As he arrived home, the cat was already walking up the driveway.

The next day, he decided to drop the cat forty blocks away, but the same thing happened. He kept on increasing the number of blocks, but the cat kept on coming home before him.

At last he decided to drive a few miles away, turn right, then left, past the bridge, then right again and another right, and so on and so on, until he reached what he thought was the perfect spot, and pushed the cat out of the door. Hours later, the man called his wife at home and asked her, 'Jen, is the cat there?'

'Yes, of course. Why do you ask?' answered the wife.

Frustrated, the man said, 'Put him on the phone. I'm lost and I need directions.'

Children

The bride said she wanted three children, while the young husband said two would be enough for him.

They discussed this discrepancy for a few minutes until the husband thought he'd put an end to things by saying boldly, 'After our second child, I'll just have a vasectomy.'

Without a moment's hesitation, the bride retorted, 'Well, I hope you'll love the third one just as if it's your own.'

A couple had been married for 45 years and had raised a brood of 11 children and were blessed with 22 grandchildren. When asked the secret for staying together all that time, the wife replied, 'Many years ago we made a promise to each other: The first one to pack up and leave has to take all the kids.'

Frank was a happily married man who had only one complaint: his wife, Myra, was always nursing sick birds.

One cold November evening he came home to find a raven with a splint on its beak sitting in his favourite chair. On the dining-room table there was a feverish eagle pecking at an aspirin tablet, while in the kitchen Myra was comforting a shivering wren.

Frank dropped his briefcase and strode over to where his wife was towelling down the cold little bird. 'Myra!' he shouted. 'I can't take it any more! We've got to get rid of all of these —'

Myra held up her hand and cut him off in mid sentence. 'Please, dear,' she said. 'Not in front of the chilled wren!'

Choices

Choose your
love, then love
your choice.

Anon

I have no way of knowing whether or not you married the wrong person, but I do know that many people have a lot of wrong ideas about marriage and what it takes to make that marriage happy and successful. I'll be the first to admit that it's possible that you did marry the wrong person. However, if you treat the wrong person like the right person, you could well end up having married the right person after all. On the other hand, if you marry the right person, and treat that person wrong, you certainly will have ended up marrying the wrong person. I also know that it is far more important to be the right kind of person than it is to marry the right person. In short, whether you married the right or wrong person is primarily up to you.

Zig Ziglar

Christmas

1 Corinthians chapter 13 (the Christmas version)

If I decorate my house perfectly with plaid bows,
strands of twinkling lights and shiny balls,
but do not show love to my family,
I'm just another decorator.

If I slave away in the kitchen,
baking dozens of Christmas delicacies,
preparing gourmet meals
and arranging a beautifully adorned table at mealtime,
but do not show love to my family,
I'm just another cook.

If I work at a soup kitchen,
sing carols in the nursing home,
and give all that I have to charity,
but do not show love to my family,
it profits me nothing.

If I trim the spruce with shimmering angels
and crocheted snowflakes,
attend a myriad of holiday parties
and sing in the choir's cantata
but do not focus on Christ,
I have missed the point.

Love stops the cooking to hug the child.
Love sets aside the decorating to kiss the spouse.
Love is kind, though harried and tired.
Love does not envy another's home
that has coordinated Christmas china and table linens.
Love does not yell at the kids to get out of the way,
but is thankful they are there to be in the way.
Love does not give only to those who are able to give in return,
but rejoices in giving to those who cannot.
Love bears all things, believes all things,
hopes all things, and endures all things.
Love never fails.

Video games will break,
pearl necklaces will be lost,
golf clubs will rust;
but giving the gift of love will endure.

Cohabitation

*D*r Nancy Moore Clatworthy, sociologist, has been doing research on 'living together' for ten years. When she began her research, the idea of living together before committing yourself to marriage made good sense to her. Now, after scientifically analyzing the results of hundreds of surveys filled out by couples who had lived together, she opposes living together in any form. Her answers make a powerfully Christian point: only a fully committed marriage relationship is really suited to working out the best possible relationship.

Tim Stafford

Colds

*H*ow does a typical husband respond when his wife comes down with a cold?

In the first year of marriage: 'Darling, I'm really worried about my baby girl. You've got a bad sniffle, and there's no telling about these things, with all the terrible viruses going around these days. I've called the emergency doctor, and I've called your mum and she's coming to help with the cooking and cleaning.'

Second year of marriage: 'Listen, Darling, I don't like the sound of that cough and I've made an appointment with the doctor. Now you go to bed like a good girl, and I'll take care of everything.'

Third year: 'Maybe you'd better lie down, Darling. Nothing like a little rest when you're feeling lousy. I'll bring you something. Do we have any canned soup?'

Fourth year: 'Now look, Dear, be sensible. After you feed the kids, do the dishes and mop the floor, you'd better get some rest.'

Fifth year: 'Why don't you take a couple of aspirin?'

Sixth year: 'If you'd just gargle or something, instead of sitting around barking like a seal all night...'

Seventh year: 'For Pete's sake, stop sneezing! What are you trying to do, give me pneumonia?'

Commandments

Ten Commandments for Marriage

1. Thou shalt not take thy partner for granted.
2. Thou shalt not expect perfection of each other.
3. Thou shalt be patient, loving, understanding, kind and true.
4. Thou shalt tend the garden of love daily.
5. Thou shalt take great care that thy partner's trust shall never be violated or diminished in any way.
6. Thou shalt not forget thy wedding vows, remembering especially those important words, *'for better or worse.'*
7. Thou shalt not hide thy true feelings. Mutual love provides a bright sunlit room where things of the heart can be discussed freely and without fear.
8. Thou shalt always respect each other as individuals. Degrading words and a sharp tongue cause grave distortions. Endearing terms ennoble, lift up and engender peace.
9. Thou shalt give thy marriage room to grow. Both partners should be willing to face the future together with confidence and trust; today is a better day for them than yesterday, and tomorrow will find them closer still.
10. Thou shalt through all thy days reverence God thy Creator, never forgetting that it is he who made you one.

"You can skip the part about '4 bitters for worse', vicar,
as I think he's already done that in the pub."

Commitment

> I n the consumer culture of marriage, commitments last as long as the other person is meeting our needs. We still believe in commitment, because we know that committed relationships are good for us, but powerful voices coming from inside and outside tell us that we are suckers if we settle for less than we think we need and deserve in our marriage. Most baby boomers and their offspring carry in our heads the internalized voice of the consumer culture – to encourage us to stop working so hard or to get out of a marriage that is not meeting our current emotional needs.
>
> *Bill Doherty*

This remarkable true story of lifelong marital commitment was published in a recent Ann Landers column in the States:

Dear Ann Landers

I'm going to tell you about a love story that I witness every time I go to the nursing home to see my husband, who has Alzheimer's disease. Unfortunately, I know firsthand how this terrible illness affects family members, but I would like the world to know what love really is.

I see a man who, I understand, has spent the last eight years caring for his wife, who has Alzheimer's. They have been married over fifty years. He cooks and feeds her every bite of food she eats. He has bathed her and dressed her every day all these years. They have no other family. She lost a baby at birth, and they never had any more children.

I cannot describe the tenderness and love that man shows for his wife. She is unable to recognize anyone, including him. The only things she shows any interest in are two baby dolls. They are never out of her hands.

I observed him when I parked my car beside his the other day. He sat in his old pickup truck for a few minutes, then he patted down what little hair he had, straightened the threadbare collar of his shirt and looked in the mirror for a final check before going in to see his wife. It was as if he were courting her. They have been partners all these years and have seen each other under all kinds of circumstances, yet he carefully groomed himself before he called on his wife, who wouldn't even know him.

Communication

A little girl and a little boy were at nursery school one day. The girl approached the boy and said, 'Hey Billy, want to play house?'

He said, 'OK! What do you want me to do?'

Sally replied, 'I want you to communicate your feelings.'

'Communicate my feelings?' said a bewildered Billy. 'I have no idea what that means.'

The little girl nodded and said, 'Perfect. You can be the husband.'

A couple attended marriage counselling to resolve communication problems. The fighting and bickering during the session were so bad that the counsellor called for a 'time out' and told them he was ending the session early.

But he had an assignment for the husband. 'John,' the counsellor said, 'you're an athletic guy... here's what I want you to do. I want you to jog 10 miles every day for the next 30 days. At the end of the 30 days call me and let me know how things are going.'

John agreed. At the end of the 30 days, John called the counsellor, very excited.

'I did just as you said and I have never felt better in my life!' he exclaimed over the phone.

'Great!' replied the counsellor. 'And how's your wife?'

John paused and then replied with agitated dismay, 'How should I know? I'm 300 miles from home!'

A psychiatrist asks a lot of expensive questions your wife asks for nothing.

Joey Adams

A couple were at a party chatting with some friends, and the subject of marriage counselling came up. 'Oh, we'll never need that. My husband and I have a great relationship,' the wife explained. 'He has a degree in Communications, and I have a degree in Theatre Arts. He communicates really well, and I just act like I'm listening.'

Ultimately the bond of all companionship, whether in marriage or in friendship, is conversation.

Oscar Wilde

Communicating frequently and intimately is the best prescription for a successful marriage.

Anon

When marrying, ask yourself this question:
Do you believe that you will be able to converse well
with this person into your old age? Everything
else in marriage is transitory.

Friedrich Nietzsche

A husband and his wife were having some disagreements and were giving each other the silent treatment. The next day, the man realized that he would need his wife to wake him at 5 a.m. for an early morning business flight.

Not wanting to be the first to break the silence (and lose!), he wrote on a piece of paper, 'Please wake me at 5 a.m.'

The next morning the man woke up, only to discover that it was 7 a.m. and he had missed his flight. Furious, he was about to go and see why his wife hadn't woken him, when he noticed a piece of paper by the bed.

The paper said, 'It is 5 a.m. Wake up.'

Before marriage, a man declares that he would lay down his life to serve you; after marriage, he won't even lay down his newspaper to talk to you.

Helen Rowland

Marriage is one long conversation, checkered with disputes.

Robert Louis Stevenson

Companionship

There is no greater happiness for a man than approaching a door at the end of a day knowing someone on the other side of that door is waiting for the sound of his footsteps.

Ronald Reagan

After all these years, I see that I was mistaken about Eve in the beginning; it is better to live outside the Garden with her than inside it without her.

Mark Twain

Don't marry the person you think you can live with; marry only the individual you think you can't live without.

James C. Dobson

Compatibility

What counts in making a
happy marriage is not so
much how compatible you are,
but how you deal with
incompatibility.

Leo Tolstoy

When asked his secret of love, being
married fifty-four years to the same
person, he said, 'Ruth and I are
happily incompatible.'

Billy Graham

As their wedding day approached, a young couple grew apprehensive. Each had a problem they had never before shared with anyone, not even each other.

The groom-to-be decided to ask his father for advice. 'Dad,' he said, I'm concerned about the success of my marriage. I love my fiancée very much, but I have smelly feet. I'm afraid that my future wife will find them, and me, disgusting.'

'No problem,' said his father, 'All you have to do is wash your feet as often as possible and always wear socks, even to bed.'

The young man thought this sounded like a workable solution.

Likewise, the bride-to-be decided to take her problem to her mother. 'Mum,' she said, 'when I wake up in the morning my breath is truly awful!'

Her mother advised, 'In the morning, get straight out of bed, head for the bathroom, and brush your teeth. Don't say a word until you've brushed them – not a word!'

The bride-to-be thought the suggestion was certainly worth a try.

The loving couple was finally married in a beautiful ceremony. Not forgetting the advice each had received – he with his perpetual socks and she with her morning silence – they managed quite well.

About six months later, shortly before dawn, the husband woke up horrified to discover that one of his socks had come off during the night. Fearful of the consequences, he frantically started searching the bed. This, of course, woke his bride.

Without thinking, she blurted out, 'What on earth are you doing?'

'Oh no!' he gasped as he recoiled in shock. 'You've swallowed my sock!'

Compliments

Try praising
your wife – even if it
does frighten her at first.

Billy Sunday

Congratulations

Congratulations on the termination of your isolation, and may I express an appreciation of your determination to end the desperation and frustration which has caused you so much consternation in giving you the inspiration to make a combination to bring an accumulation to the population.

Courting

Once there was a millionaire who collected live alligators. He kept them in the pool at the back of his mansion. He also had a beautiful daughter who was single. One day he decided to throw a huge party, and during the party he announced, 'My dear guests... I have a proposition to every man here. I will give one million dollars or my daughter to the man who can swim across this pool full of alligators and emerge alive!'

As soon as he finished his last word, there was the sound of a large splash! There was one man in the pool swimming with all his might and screaming out of fear. The crowd cheered him on. Finally, he made it to the other side with only a torn shirt and some minor injuries.

The millionaire was impressed. He said, 'My boy, that was incredible! Fantastic! I didn't think it could be done! Well, I must keep my end of the bargain. Do you want my daughter or the one million dollars?'

The man said, 'Listen, I don't want your money or your daughter! I want the person who pushed me into that pool!'

Listen! My lover!
Look! Here he comes,
leaping across the mountains,
bounding over the hills.
My lover is like a gazelle or a young stag.
Look! There he stands behind our wall,
gazing through the windows,
peering through the lattice.
My lover spoke and said to me,
'Arise, my darling,
my beautiful one, and come with me.
See! The winter is past;
the rains are over and gone.
Flowers appear on the earth;
the season of singing has come,
the cooing of doves
is heard in our land.
The fig tree forms its early fruit;
the blossoming vines spread their fragrance.
Arise, come, my darling;
my beautiful one, come with me.'

Song of Songs 2:8–13, NIV

An Austrian anthropologist named Weizl, who lived for a time among the natives of northern Siberia, was frequently accosted by giggling young maidens who showed up at his door and pelted him with freshly killed lice. Eventually Weizl learned that among northern Siberians, lice-throwing was a customary way for a woman to declare her interest in a man and indicate that she was available for marriage.

Christian boys' chat-up lines

1. 'Nice Bible.'
2. 'Is this pew taken?'
3. 'I just don't feel called to celibacy.'
4. 'For you I would slay two Goliaths.'
5. 'I would go through more than the book of Job for you.'
6. 'Shall we tithe?'
7. 'At points in my life I have been referred to as Samson.'
8. 'The Bible says, "Give drink to those who are thirsty, and feed the hungry." So how about dinner?'
9. 'I didn't believe in predestination until tonight.'
10. 'I believe one of my ribs belongs to you.'

Six ways to learn everything you ever need to know about a man before you decide to marry him:

1. Watch him drive in heavy traffic.
2. Play tennis with him.
3. Listen to him talk to his mother when he doesn't know you're listening.
4. See how he treats those who serve him (waiters, maids).
5. Notice what he's willing to spend his money to buy.
6. Look at his friends.

And if you still can't make up your mind, then look at his shoes. A man who keeps his shoes in good repair generally tends to the rest of his life too.

Lois Wyse

Courtship is like looking at the beautiful photos in a seed catalogue.

Anon

A man walks up to the bar with an ostrich behind him and, as he sits, the bartender comes over and asks for their order.

The man says, 'I'll have a beer.' Turning to the ostrich, he says, 'What's yours?'

'I'll have a beer too,' says the ostrich.

The bartender pours the beer and says, 'That will be £4.40, please.'

The man reaches into his pocket and pulls out the exact change for payment.

The next day, the man and the ostrich come again and the man says, 'I'll have a beer,' and the ostrich says, 'I'll have the same.'

Once again the man reaches into his pocket and pays with the exact change.

This becomes a routine until, late one evening, the two enter again.

'The usual?' asks the bartender.

'Well, it's nearly closing time, so I'll have a large Scotch,' says the man.

'Same for me,' says the ostrich.

'That will be £6.20,' says the bartender.

Once again the man pulls the exact change out of his pocket and places it on the bar. The bartender can't hold back his curiosity any longer.

'Excuse me, sir. How do you manage to always come up with the exact change out of your pocket every time?'

'Well,' says the man, 'several years ago I was cleaning the attic and I found an old lamp. When I rubbed it, a genie appeared and offered me two wishes. My first wish was that if I ever had to pay for anything, I could just put my hand in my pocket and the right amount of money would always be there.'

'That's brilliant!' says the bartender. 'Most people would wish for a million dollars or something, but you'll always be as rich as you want for as long as you live!'

'That's right! Whether it's a gallon of milk or a Rolls Royce, the exact money is always there,' says the man.

The bartender asks, 'One other thing, sir... What's with the ostrich?'

The man replies, 'My second wish was for a chick with long legs.'

A young man said to his father at breakfast one morning, 'Dad, I'm going to get married.'

'How do you know you're ready to get married?' asked the father. 'Are you in love?'

'I certainly am,' said the son.

'How do you know you're in love?' asked the father.

'Last night as I was kissing my girlfriend goodnight, her dog bit me and I didn't feel the pain until I got home.'

"Matron, would you like to deal with any malingerers in the waiting room, please?"

A boy is about to go on his first date, and is nervous about what to talk about. He asks his father for advice.

The father replies: 'My son, there are three subjects that always work. These are food, family and philosophy.'

The boy picks up his date and they go to a McDonald's. Burgers in front of them, they stare at each other for a long time, as the boy's nervousness builds. He remembers his father's advice, and chooses the first topic. He asks the girl, 'Do you like spinach?'

She says 'No,' and the silence returns.

After a few more uncomfortable minutes, the boy thinks of his father's suggestion and turns to the second item on the list. He asks, 'Do you have a brother?'

Again, the girl says 'No,' and there is silence once again.

The boy then plays his last card. He thinks of his father's advice and asks the girl the following question: 'If you had a brother, would he like spinach?'

An elderly woman died recently. Having never married, she requested that her coffin should be carried by women, not by men.

In her handwritten instructions for her funeral, she wrote: 'They wouldn't take me out while I was alive, so I certainly don't want them to take me out when I'm dead!'

Death

A man died and his wife phoned the newspaper to place an obituary. She said, 'This is what I want to print: "Bernie is dead."'

The man at the newspaper said, 'But for £25 you are allowed to print six words.'

The woman answered, 'OK. Then print: "Bernie is dead. Toyota for sale."'

How would you like to be married to Vanda Vorotova? She rivals Liz Taylor and Zza Zza Gabor in the frequency-of-marriage stakes. Vanda has been married eight times. But there is a major difference between Vanda, Liz Taylor and Zza Zza. Vanda's husbands have a strange habit of dying.

Husband number 1 died when he fell from their flat.

Husband number 2 was the lucky one – she left him while he was still alive.

Husband number 3 was electrocuted when the TV he was watching fell into the bath he was watching it from.

Husband number 4 died from a sudden illness.

Husband number 5 died of unexplained causes.

Husband number 6 died of a medical overdose.

Husband number 7 died in his sleep.

When husband number 8 died from axe wounds, the police began to get suspicious. Vanda confessed to his murder when his blood was found on her jacket, and the previously unsuspecting police are now investigating the deaths of her other husbands.

A man was crying over a gravestone, saying, 'Why did you die? Why did you die?'

Another man asked him, 'Did your mother just die?'

'No.'

'Your father?'

'No.' He continued, 'Oh, why did you die?'

'Well, who died?'

'This was my wife's first husband.'

Consider the case of the Illinois man who left the snow-filled streets of Chicago for a vacation in Florida. His wife was on a business trip and was planning to meet him there the next day. When he reached his hotel, he decided to send his wife a quick email. Unable to find the scrap of paper on which he had written her email address, he did his best to type it in from memory. Unfortunately, he missed one letter, and his note was directed instead to a preacher's wife, whose husband had passed away only the day before.

When the grieving widow checked her emails, she took one look at the monitor and let out a piercing scream, and fell to the floor in a dead faint. At the sound, her family rushed into the room and saw this note on the screen:

> *Dearest Wife,*
> *Just got checked in. Everything prepared for your arrival tomorrow.*
> *PS: Sure is hot down here.*

My grandparents were married for over half a century, and played their own special game from the time they had met each other. The goal of their game was to write the word 'shmily' in a surprise place for the other to find. They took turns leaving 'shmily' around the house, and as soon as one of them discovered it, it was their turn to hide it once more.

They dragged 'shmily' with their fingers through the sugar and flour containers to await whoever was preparing the next meal. They smeared it in the dew on the windows overlooking the patio. 'Shmily' was written in the steam left on the mirror after a hot shower, where it would reappear, bath after bath. At one point, my Grandmother even unrolled an entire roll of toilet paper to leave 'shmily' on the very last sheet.

There was no end to the places 'shmily' would pop up. Little notes with 'shmily' scribbled hurriedly were found on dashboards and car seats, or taped to steering wheels. The notes were stuffed inside shoes and left under pillows. 'Shmily' was written in the dust upon the mantel and traced in the ashes of the fireplace. This mysterious word was as much a part of my grandparents' house as the furniture.

But there was a dark cloud in my grandparents' life: my Grandmother had breast cancer. The disease had first appeared ten years earlier. As always, Grandpa was with her every step of the way. He comforted her in their yellow room, painted that way so that she could always be surrounded by sunshine, even when she was too sick to go outside.

Now the cancer was again attacking her body. With the help of a cane and my Grandfather's steady hand, they went to church every morning. But my Grandmother grew steadily weaker until, finally, she could not leave the house any more. For a while, Grandpa would go to church alone, praying to God to watch over his wife. Then one day, what we all dreaded finally happened. Grandma was gone.

'Shmily.' It was scrawled in yellow on the pink ribbons of my Grandmother's funeral bouquet. As the crowd thinned and the last mourners turned to leave, my aunts, uncles, cousins and other family members came forward and gathered around Grandma one last time. Grandpa stepped up to my Grandmother's casket and, taking a shaky breath, he began to sing to her. Through his tears and grief, the song came, a deep and throaty lullaby.

Shaking with my own sorrow, I will never forget that moment. For I knew that, although I couldn't begin to fathom the depth of their love, I had been privileged to witness its unmatched beauty.

S-H-M-I-L-Y: See How Much I Love You.

The author and lecturer Leo Buscaglia once talked about a contest he was asked to judge. The purpose of the contest was to find the most caring child. The winner was a four-year-old child whose next-door neighbour was an elderly gentleman who had recently lost his wife.

Upon seeing the man cry, the little boy went into the old gentleman's garden, climbed onto his lap, and just sat there.

When his mother asked him what he had said to the neighbour, the little boy said, 'Nothing. I just helped him cry.'

The German poet Heinrich Heine bequeathed his entire estate to his widow on the condition that she remarry — 'So at least one other man will regret my death.'

Divorce

Love, the quest;
marriage, the conquest;
divorce, the inquest.

Helen Rowland

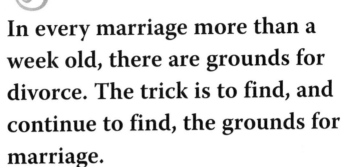

In every marriage more than a week old, there are grounds for divorce. The trick is to find, and continue to find, the grounds for marriage.

Robert Anderson

It is not marriage that fails; it is people that fail. All that marriage does is to show people up.

Harry Emerson Fosdick

I'm a great housekeeper.
I get divorced.
I keep the house.

Zsa Zsa Gabor

My husband and I divorced over religious differences.
He thought he was God, and I didn't.
Anon

"Well, there's your big bang – now go create."

Dogs

I never married because there was no need. I have three pets at home which answer the same purpose as a husband. I have a dog that growls every morning, a parrot that swears all afternoon, and a cat that comes home late at night.

Marie Corelli

John got off the elevator on the fiftieth floor and nervously knocked on his blind date's door. She opened it and was as beautiful and charming as everyone had said.

'I'll be ready in a few minutes,' she said. 'Why don't you play with Spot, my dog, while you're waiting? He does wonderful tricks. He rolls over, shakes hands, sits up and if you make a hoop with your arms, he'll jump through.'

The dog followed John onto the balcony and started rolling over. John made a hoop with his arms and Spot jumped through – over the balcony railing. Just then John's date walked out.

'Isn't Spot the cutest, happiest dog you've ever seen?'

'To tell the truth,' he replied, 'Spot seemed a little depressed to me!'

Driving

The other day my wife and I were discussing formal and informal prayer. I said, 'I do some of my best praying while I'm driving.'

And my wife agreed by saying, 'I, too, do my best praying while you're driving.'

Encouragement

> ## Be presidents of each other's fan clubs.
>
> *Tony Heath*

Excuses

A senior citizen drove his brand-new BMW Z3 convertible out of the car salesroom. Taking off down the motorway, he floored it to 90 m.p.h., enjoying the wind blowing through what little hair he had left.

'Amazing!' he thought as he flew down the M40, enjoying pushing the pedal to the metal even more. Looking in his rear-view mirror, he saw a police car behind him, blue lights flashing and siren blaring.

'I can get away from him – no problem!' thought the elderly nutcase as he floored it to 110 m.p.h., then 120, then 130.

Suddenly, he thought, 'What on earth am I doing? I'm too old for this nonsense!' So he pulled over to the side of the road and waited for the police car to catch up with him.

Pulling in behind him, the police officer walked up to the driver's side of the BMW, looked at his watch and said, 'Sir, my shift ends in ten minutes. Today is Friday and I'm taking off for the weekend. If you can give me a reason why you were speeding that I've never heard before, I'll let you go.'

The man looked very seriously at the policeman and replied, 'Years ago, my wife ran off with a policeman. I thought you were bringing her back.'

'Have a good day, sir,' said the policeman.

Faithfulness

As he lay on his deathbed, the man confided to his wife, 'I cannot die without telling you the truth. I cheated on you throughout our whole marriage. All those nights when I told you I was working late, I was with other women – I've slept with dozens of them.'

His wife looked at him calmly and said, 'Why do you think I gave you the poison?'

The grass looks greener… but it's Astroturf.

From a report entitled,
'Does Divorce Make People Happy?'

If the grass looks greener on the other side of the fence, it's because they take better care of it.

Cecil Selig

The secret of staying married, according to Jon Bon Jovi: 'My wife tells me that if I ever decide to leave, she is coming with me.'

More and more people seem to forget Henry Ford's sage advice when asked, on his fiftieth wedding anniversary, for his rule for marital bliss and longevity. He replied, 'Just the same as in the automobile business – stick to one model.'

A man went into a photography shop with a framed picture of his girlfriend. He wanted another copy of the photo. This involved removing it from the frame. The assistant noticed the inscription on the back of the photograph:

My dearest Tom, I love you with all my heart. I love you more and more each day. I will love you forever and ever. I am yours for all eternity. *Diane.*

And there was a PS: 'If we ever break up, I want this picture back.'

> Bad marriages don't cause infidelity; infidelity causes bad marriages.
>
> *Frank Pittman*

> Fidelity is the single most important element in solidly enduring marriages.
>
> *Frank Pittman*

When Adam stayed out very late for a few nights, Eve became upset. 'You're running around with other women,' she charged.

'You're being unreasonable,' Adam responded. 'You're the only woman on earth.'

The quarrel continued until Adam fell asleep, only to be awakened by someone poking him in the chest. It was Eve.

'What do you think you're doing?' Adam demanded.

'Counting your ribs,' said Eve.

We've all heard of the US Air Force's ultra-high-security, super-secret base in Nevada, known simply as 'Area 51'. Late one afternoon, the Air Force folks out at Area 51 were very surprised to see a Cessna landing at their 'secret' base. They immediately impounded the aircraft and hauled the pilot into an interrogation room.

The pilot's story was that he took off from Vegas, got lost, and spotted the base just as he was about to run out of fuel. The Air Force started a full FBI background check on the pilot and held him overnight during the investigation. By the next day, they were finally convinced that the pilot really was lost and wasn't a spy. They refuelled his aeroplane, gave him a terrifying 'you-did-not-see-a-base' briefing, complete with threats of spending the rest of his life in prison, told him Vegas was so many kilometres away on such-and-such a heading, and sent him on his way.

The next day, to the total disbelief of the Air Force, the same Cessna showed up again. Once again, the MPs surrounded the plane, only this time there were two people in it. The same pilot jumped out and said, 'Do anything you want to me, but my wife is in the plane, and since I can't tell her where I was last night, you have to!'

I'm tempted to go to all the buildings downtown and put up a sign, 'DANGER ZONE: Men and Women at Work'. Today's workplace is the most common breeding ground for affairs. It's the proximity and collegiality, the intimacy of working together, not bad marriages, that is the slippery slope to infidelity.

Shirley Glass

*M*arty wakes up with a killer hangover. He forces himself to open his eyes, and the first things he sees are a couple of aspirin and a glass of water on the side table. He sits up and sees his clothes in front of him, clean and pressed.

He takes the aspirin and notices a note on the table: 'Honey, breakfast is on the stove. I left early to go shopping. Love you.'

He goes to the kitchen and, sure enough, there is a hot breakfast and the morning newspaper. His son is also at the table, eating.

Marty asks, 'Son, what happened last night?'

His son says, 'Well, you came home at 3 a.m., drunk and delirious. Broke some furniture, puked in the hallway, and gave yourself a black eye when you stumbled into the door.'

Confused, Marty asks, 'So, why is everything in order and so clean, and why is breakfast on the table waiting for me?'

His son replies, 'Oh, that! Mum dragged you to the bedroom, and when she tried to take your trousers off, you said, "Lady, leave me alone, I'm married"!'

INTERVIEWER: 'For so long you were the poster boy for American bachelorhood. Now that you've settled into a marriage, do you find monogamy difficult?'

WARREN BEATTY: 'No. I would imagine that marriage without it is difficult.'

New York Times Sunday Magazine, 1 October 2006

What we really need is a time machine so that people entering into an affair could flash forward and see themselves, their kids, their lives at the other end of this 'tunnel of love' — at the end of the fun.

Diane Sollee

Families

> Sally came home with her new fur coat. When her daughter saw the coat she yelled, 'Mum, you should be ashamed of yourself, wearing a fur coat! Don't you realize that a poor dumb animal has suffered for that?'
>
> Sally looked at her daughter angrily and shouted out, 'Don't you dare talk about your father like that!'

An elderly man in Florida calls his son in New York. The father says to the son, 'I hate to tell you, but we've got some troubles here in the house. Your mother and I can't stand each other any more, and we're getting a divorce. I've had it! I want to live out the rest of my years in peace. I'm telling you now, so you and your sister won't go into shock later when I move out.'

He hangs up, and the son immediately calls his sister and tells her the news. The sister says, 'I'll handle this!'

She calls Florida and says to her father, 'Don't do *anything* until we get there! We'll be there Wednesday night.'

The father agrees. He hangs up the phone and hollers to his wife, 'Okay, they're coming for Thanksgiving. Now, what are we going to tell them for Christmas?'

Fathers-in-Law

When Leslie brought home her fiancé to meet her parents, her father invited the young man into his study to find out more about him.

'What are your plans?' he asked Joseph.

'I'm a scholar of the Torah,' Joseph replied.

'Well, that's admirable,' Leslie's father replied. 'But what will you do to provide a nice house for my daughter?'

'I will study, and God will surely provide for us,' Joseph explained.

'And how will you buy her a nice engagement ring?'

'I will study hard, and God will provide for us.'

'And children?' asked the father. 'How will you support children?'

'Don't worry, sir. God will provide,' replied the fiancé.

The conversation continued in much the same fashion. After Joseph and Leslie had left, her mother asked her father what he had found out. The father answered, 'Well, he has no job and no plans, but the good news is that he thinks I'm God.'

Fire

To keep a fire burning brightly, there's one easy rule: keep the logs together, near enough to keep warm and far enough apart for breathing room. Good fire, good marriage. Same rule.

Dear Abby

Some months ago, you printed a letter from a reader who was disturbed that the spark was gone from her marriage. I asked my husband whether the spark is gone from our eighteen-year marriage. His response: 'A spark lasts only a second. It lights a fire. When the flame burns down, we are left with the hottest part of the fire, the embers, which burn the longest and keep the fire alive.'

Anon

Marriage is like a gas stove. Even if the burners aren't on all the time, you've always got to keep the pilot light lit.

Brian, a husband giving advice

Food

Why are married women heavier than single women? Because single women come home, see what's in the fridge and go to bed, whereas married women come home, see what's in the bed and go to the fridge!

There was a couple, eighty-five years old, who had been married for sixty years. Though they were far from rich, they managed to get by because they watched their pennies. They were both in very good health, largely due to the wife's insistence on healthy foods and exercise for the last decade.

One day, their good health didn't help when they went on a rare vacation and their plane crashed, sending them off to Heaven. They reached the pearly gates, and St Peter escorted them inside.

He took them to a beautiful mansion, furnished in gold and fine silks, with a fully stocked kitchen and a waterfall in the master bathroom. A maid could be seen hanging their favourite clothes in the closet. They gasped in astonishment when he said, 'Welcome to Heaven. This will be your home now.'

The old man asked St Peter how much all this was going to cost.

'Why, nothing,' Peter replied. 'Remember, this is your reward in Heaven.'

The old man looked out the window, and right there, he saw a championship golf course, finer and more beautiful than any ever built on earth.

'What are the greens fees?' grumbled the old man.

'This is Heaven,' St Peter replied. 'You can play for free, every day.'

Next they went to the clubhouse and saw the lavish buffet lunch, with every imaginable cuisine laid out before them, from seafood to steaks to exotic desserts, with free-flowing beverages.

'Don't even ask,' said St Peter to the man. 'This is Heaven – it's all free for you to enjoy.'

The old man looked around and glanced nervously at his wife. 'Well, where are the low-fat and low-cholesterol foods, and the decaffeinated tea?' he asked.

'That's the best part,' St Peter replied. 'You can eat and drink as much as you like of whatever you like, and you will never get fat or sick. This is Heaven!'

The old man pushed, 'No gym to work out at?'

'Not unless you want to,' was the answer.

'No testing my sugar or blood pressure or...'

'Never again. All you do here is enjoy yourself.'

The old man glared at his wife and said, 'You and your stupid bran muffins. We could have been here ten years ago!'

Forgiveness

A couple who had been married for fifteen years began having more than usual disagreements. They wanted to make their marriage work and agreed on an idea the wife had. For one month they planned to put notes in a 'Fault' box. The boxes would provide a place to let the other know about daily irritations.

The wife was diligent in her efforts and approach: 'leaving the top off the jam jar'; 'wet towels on the bathroom floor'; 'dirty socks not in laundry basket', and on and on until the end of the month.

After dinner, at the end of the month, they exchanged boxes. The husband reflected on what he had done wrong. Then the wife opened her box and began reading. The notes were all the same. The message on each slip was: 'I love you!'

> *Once a woman has forgiven a man, she must not reheat his sins for breakfast.*
>
> Marlene Dietrich

> *Stephen Covey was once asked about how to forgive someone who has committed adultery. He said the question made him think of the old prayer, 'Oh Lord, let me forgive those who sin differently than I do.'*

A good marriage
is the union of two
forgivers.

Ruth Graham

On her golden wedding anniversary, my grandmother revealed the secret of her long and happy marriage:

'On my wedding day, I decided to choose ten of my husband's faults which, for the sake of our marriage, I would overlook,' she explained.

A guest asked her to name some of the faults. 'To tell the truth,' she replied, 'I never did get around to listing them. But whenever my husband did something that made me hopping mad, I would say to myself, "Lucky for him that's one of the ten."'

Before you marry, keep your two eyes open; after you marry, shut one.

Jamaican proverb

"One eye open for the camera NOW Derek!"

Marriage is
three parts love and
seven parts
forgiveness of sins.

Langdon Mitchell

Friendship

**Marriage,
ultimately, is the
practice of becoming
passionate friends.**

Harville Hendrix

*It is not a lack of love,
but a lack of friendship that
makes unhappy marriages.*

Freidrich Nietzsche

Gaps

I got gaps; you got gaps; we fill each other's gaps.

Rocky (the film character)

Generosity

A good marriage is a contest of generosity.

Diane Sawyer

Gifts

A fellow was very much in love with a beautiful girl. One day she told him that the next day was her birthday. He told her he would send her a bouquet of roses... one for each year of her life.

That evening he called the local florist and ordered twenty-one roses, with instructions that they be delivered first thing the next morning.

As the florist was preparing the order, he decided that since the young man was such a good customer, he would put an extra dozen roses in the bouquet.

The fellow never did find out what made the girl so angry with him.

Madame Prelle had become very fed up with neighbours parking outside her home. After weeks of pleading, she arose before dawn one morning and set to work on the gleaming maroon Citroen in front of her gate.

Gleefully she scratched the paintwork with a wire brush, poured litres of gloss paint over the roof and slashed the tyres, before returning to her bed, deeply satisfied.

She was awakened later by her husband who wanted to announce his tenth anniversary present to her... a brand-new maroon Citroen.

A group of men are sitting in a sauna discussing business and stocks when suddenly a mobile phone rings.

'Hi honey, are you at the club?' asks the caller.

'Yes, dear.'

'Honey, you won't believe this, but I'm standing in front of Giovanni's, and there's a beautiful mink on sale in the window.'

'How much is it, dear?'

'They're giving it away. Only £5,000! Can you believe it?'

'But you already have fur coats.'

'Please, dear – it's absolutely exquisite!'

'Fine, fine – go ahead and buy it.'

'Thank you, sweetheart. Oh, by the way, I passed by the Mercedes dealership this morning and saw their new convertible. It was to die for! I talked to the salesman and the one in the showroom is brand new, leather seats, power everything, gold coloured. What do you think?'

'Honey, come on – we already have cars!'

'You promised me that I could get a convertible!'

'How much is it?'

'You won't believe it, but he said he'd let us have it for £85,000, fully loaded with all the options!'

'OK, OK, go ahead and purchase it.'

'I love you, you're the best husband a wife could ask for. I hope I'm not pushing it, but remember the trip we took to Paris? Remember the Browns' place with the swimming pool and the tennis courts? It's on the market to be sold. I saw it this morning at the estate agent's. If we bought it, we would have a perfect place to stay during the cold winter months!'

'I had actually thought about it. You say it's on the market?'

'Really, you were actually thinking about it? Can I go and make an offer on it? The price isn't very high, and it would be perfect for our type of lifestyle!'

'How much are they asking for?'

'Only £425,000 sweetheart. It's a steal!'

'I guess we've got money put away. Go ahead and make an offer, but no more than £415,000.'

'This is turning out to be a great day! Can't wait to see you tonight to celebrate!'

'See you tonight, dear.'

The man ends the call and asks, 'So, whose phone is this?'

Presents you don't want to give your wife

10. A car-wash kit.
9. A table saw.
8. Two all-day passes to Comet's Home Theatre Installation Seminar.
7. A bottle of engine oil.
6. A five-year subscription to *Sports Illustrated*.
5. A custom-engraved cricket-bat.
4. An outboard motor for a fishing boat.
3. The *Rambo* trilogy on DVD.
2. A new satellite dish with a sports package.
1. A three-year membership of Weight Watchers.

Presents you don't want to give your husband

10. The *Anne of Avonlea/Anne of Green Gables* Collector's Edition with 74 minutes of extra footage.
9. Any knick-knack.
8. Tickets to the ballet.
7. Another new tie.
6. A Body Shop soap basket.
5. Teddy-bear pyjamas.
4. A vacuum cleaner.
3. A weekend seminar on 'Getting in Touch With Your Feelings'.
2. A pair of fuzzy bunny slippers.
1. A nose- and ear-hair trimmer (OK, well maybe).

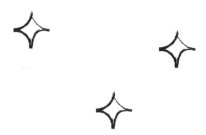

Looking for a gift or just a unique way to say 'I love you?' What do you give when his dresser is full of cologne and you're both on diets? When she thinks flowers die too soon, and you've already spent next month's pay-cheque? Here are 21 great inexpensive ways to tell the love of your life just how much you care:

1. Make a homemade card with a picture of the two of you on the cover. Get ideas for a verse by spending a few minutes browsing through a card shop.
2. Write a poem. It doesn't have to rhyme.
3. Send a love letter listing the reasons 'Why I love you so much.'
4. Pledge your love for a lifetime. Write it in calligraphy or design it on a computer and print it out on parchment paper and have it framed.
5. Plan a surprise lunch, complete with picnic basket, sparkling grape juice and goblets.
6. Bake a giant cookie and write 'I love you' with heart-shaped frosting. (Don't worry about the calories – it's not for eating!)
7. Make a coupon book and include coupons for a back rub, a compromise when you're about to lose an argument, a listening ear when needed, and doing the dishes when the other cooks.
8. Kidnap the car for a thorough washing and valeting.
9. Design your personal crest, combining symbols that are meaningful to both of you.
10. Compose a love song.
11. Arrange for someone to sing a favourite love song to you and your love when you're together.
12. Call a radio station and have them announce a love message from you and make sure your love is listening at the right time.
13. Make a big sign such as: 'I Love You, Kristi. Love, Joe' and put it in front of your house or her apartment complex for the world to see.
14. Buy favourite fruits that aren't in season, like a basket of strawberries or blueberries.
15. Hide little love notes in the car, or a coat pocket, or a desk.
16. Place a love message in the 'personal' section of the classified ads in your local paper.
17. Florist flowers aren't the only way to say 'I love you.' Pluck a single flower and write a message about how its beauty reminds you of your love. For greater impact, have it delivered at work.
18. Prepare a surprise candle-lit gourmet low-calorie dinner for two.
19. Write the story of the growth of your relationship from your perspective, sharing your emotions and your joys. What a treasure!
20. Make a paperweight from a smooth stone, paint it, and write a special love message on it.
21. Promise to change a habit that your love has been wanting you to change.

What *not* to buy your wife

Although the only person a man usually shops for is his wife, the whole experience is a stressful one. Many a man has felt extreme frigid temperatures for a long period based on a poor present decision. As a veteran of these wars, I'm still not sure what to buy my wife, but I'll pass on what not to buy her:

1. Don't buy anything that plugs in. Anything that requires electricity is seen as utilitarian.
2. Don't buy clothing that involves sizes. The chances are one in seven thousand that you will get her size right, and your wife will be offended the other 6,999 times. 'Do I look like a size 16?' she'll say. Too small a size doesn't cut it either: 'I haven't worn a size 8 in 20 years!'
3. Avoid all things useful. The new silver polish advertised to save hundreds of hours is not going to win you any brownie points.
4. Don't buy anything that involves weight loss or self-improvement. She'll perceive a six-month membership to a diet centre as a suggestion that's she's overweight.
5. Don't buy jewellery. The jewellery your wife wants, you can't afford. And the jewellery you can afford, she doesn't want.
6. And, guys, do not fall into the traditional trap of buying her frilly underwear. Your idea of the kind your wife should wear and what she actually wears are light years apart.
7. Finally, don't spend too much. 'How do you think we're going to afford that?' she'll ask. But don't spend too little. She won't say anything, but she'll think, 'Is that all I'm worth?'

Herb Forst

"My word, the balance on these rosewood handles really is good, isn't it?"

God

> *A braid appears to contain only two strands of hair. But it is impossible to create a braid with only two strands. If the two could be put together at all, they would quickly unravel. Herein lies the mystery: what looks like two strands requires a third. The third strand, though not immediately evident, keeps the strands tightly woven. In a Christian marriage, God's presence, like the third strand in a braid, holds husband and wife together.*
>
> *Catherine Paxton*

Gossip

One day, at a distance, a man saw his vicar hugging the wife of another church member. He was shocked. The first thing he did was tell other members of the church what he had seen, 'just between the two of us'.

That Sunday the vicar announced that one of the members of the church had suffered a terrible tragedy earlier in the week. It turned out that what the gossiping church member saw was the vicar consoling the wife.

He was so ashamed that he went to his vicar and confessed what he had done, and asked for forgiveness, which he was granted.

The vicar asked the man to do him a favour. Because he felt so guilty, he jumped at the chance.

So the vicar said to him, 'Take this feather pillow to the top of the hill in the centre of town, tear it open and release all the feathers to the wind, then come back to me when you have finished.'

The church member obliged, convinced that he knew the lesson he was being taught. When he came back to the vicar, he told him that he understood the lesson – that gossip can spread quickly and easily.

The vicar said, 'That's true, but here's the most important part of the lesson: go and pick up every feather.'

Grouchy

One woman to another
at the office:
'Did you wake up
grouchy today?'
'No, I just let him
sleep in.'

Hatred

The newspaper columnist and minister George Crane tells of a wife who came into his office full of hatred toward her husband.

'I do not only want to get rid of him, I want to get even,' she said. 'Before I divorce him, I want to hurt him as much as he has me.'

Dr Crane suggested an ingenious plan: 'Go home and act as if you really love your husband. Tell him how much he means to you. Praise him for every decent trait. Go out of your way to be as kind, considerate and generous as possible. Spare no efforts to please him, to enjoy him. Make him believe you love him. After you've convinced him of your undying love and that you cannot live without him, then drop the bomb. Tell him that you're getting a divorce. That will really hurt him.'

With revenge in her eyes, she smiled and exclaimed, 'Beautiful, beautiful. He'll be so surprised!'

And she did it with enthusiasm, acting 'as if'. For two months she showed love, kindness, listening, giving, reinforcing, sharing.

When she didn't return, Crane called her. 'Are you ready now to go through with the divorce?'

'Divorce?' she exclaimed. 'Never! I discovered I really do love him.'

Her actions had changed her feelings.

Heaven

A woman who had died found herself standing outside the Pearly Gates, being greeted by St Peter.

She asked him, 'Oh, is this place really what I think it is? It's so beautiful. Did I really make it to heaven?'

To which St Peter replied, 'Yes, my dear, these are the Gates to Heaven. But you must do one more thing before you can enter.'

The woman was very excited, and asked St Peter what she must do to pass through the gates.

'Spell a word,' St Peter replied.

'What word?' she asked.

'Any word,' answered St Peter. 'It's your choice.'

The woman promptly replied, 'Then the word I will spell is love. L-o-v-e.'

St Peter congratulated her on her good fortune to have made it to Heaven, and asked her if she would mind taking his place at the gates for a few minutes while he went to the bathroom.

'I'd be honoured,' she said, 'but what should I do if someone comes while you are gone?'

St Peter reassured her, and instructed her simply to ask any newcomers to the Pearly Gates to spell a word, as she had done.

So the woman was left sitting in St Peter's chair and watching the beautiful angels soaring around her, when lo and behold, a man approached the gates, and she realized it was her husband.

'What happened?' she cried. 'Why are you here?'

Her husband stared at her for a moment, then said, 'I was so upset when I left your funeral, I had an accident. And now I'm here! Did I really make it to Heaven?'

To which the woman replied, 'Not yet. You must spell a word first.'

'What word?' he asked.

The woman responded, 'Czechoslovakia.'

Helpfulness

One day, while a wife was working in her kitchen, a cupboard door came loose. When her husband got home, she asked him to fix it.

He told her, 'Do you see the word "carpenter" written anywhere on this shirt?'

She said 'No,' and he went on his way.

The next day, while cleaning in the basement, she found the light didn't work. She changed the light bulb and did everything she could to try to fix it, but it still wouldn't work.

When her husband got home, she asked him, 'Honey, do you think you could fix the light in the basement for me?'

He simply said, 'Do you see the word "electrician" written anywhere on this shirt?'

She said 'No,' and he went into the living room to relax.

The next day, a pipe in the kitchen began leaking. When her husband got home, she asked him to fix it for her, to which he replied, 'Do you see the word "plumber" written anywhere on my shirt?'

'No,' she said, again.

The next day, the husband returned from work and saw that everything was fixed – the pipe, the light, and even the cupboard!

He asked her, 'Who fixed all of this?'

To which she replied, 'I asked our neighbour to come over and help, and he gladly agreed.'

'Well, how did you repay him for his services?' he asked.

'Well,' she replied, 'he only asked for sex, or cookies.'

The husband thought a moment, then said, 'So what kind of cookies did you bake him?'

The wife quickly snapped back, 'Do you see "Delia Smith" written anywhere on this shirt?!'

Hen-pecked

There were three guys talking in the pub. Two of them were talking about the amount of control they had over their wives, while the third remained quiet.

After a while one of the first two turned to the third and said, 'Well, what about you? What sort of control do you have over your wife?'

The third fellow said, 'I'll tell you. Just the other night my wife came to me on her hands and knees.'

The first two guys were amazed. 'Wow! What happened then?' they asked.

The third man took a healthy swallow of his beer, sighed and said, 'She said, "Get out from under the bed and fight like a man!"'

It's Armageddon, and everyone on earth dies and waits outside the gates for judgment.

God comes and says, 'I want the men to make two lines. One line is for the men who dominated their women on earth and the other line is for the men who were dominated by their women. Also, I want all the women to go with St Peter.'

With that said and done, the next time God looks, the women are gone and there are two lines. The line of the men who were dominated by their women is thousands of miles long, and in the line of men who dominated their women, there is only one man.

God gets angry and says, 'You men should be ashamed of yourselves. I created you in my image and you were all whipped by your mates. Look at the only one of my sons who stood up and made me proud. Learn from him! Tell them, my son, how did you manage to be the only one in this line?'

And the man replies, 'I don't know. My wife told me to stand here.'

Tom had won a toy at a raffle. He called his kids together to ask which one should have the present.

'Who is the most obedient?' he asked. 'Who never talks back to mother? Who does everything she says?'

Five small voices answered in unison, 'OK, Dad, you get the toy.'

We accompanied our son and his fiancée when they met with her priest to sign some pre-wedding ceremony papers. While filling out the form, our son read aloud a few questions. When he got to the last one, which read: 'Are you entering this marriage at your own will?' he looked over at his fiancée. 'Put down "Yes,"' she said.

Lilyan van Almelo

It was a terrible night, blowing cold and rain in a most frightful manner. The streets were deserted and the local baker was just about to close up shop when a little man slipped through the door. He carried an umbrella, blown inside out, and was bundled in two sweaters and a thick coat. But even so, he still looked wet and bedraggled.

As he unwound his scarf he said to the baker, 'May I have two rolls to go, please?'

The baker said in astonishment, 'Two rolls? Nothing more?'

'That's right,' answered the little man. 'One for me and one for Bernice.'

'Bernice is your wife?' asked the baker.

'What do you think?' snapped the little man. 'Would my mother send me out on a night like this?'

Holidays

A couple were going on holiday, standing in line waiting to check their bags at the airline counter.

The husband said to the wife, 'I wish we had brought the piano.'

The wife said, 'Why? We've got sixteen bags already!'

The husband said, 'Yes, I know – but the tickets are on the piano!'

Honeymoons

A young couple were married and then embarked on their honeymoon. When they returned, the bride ran to the phone and called her mother, who asked, 'How was your honeymoon, dear?'

'Oh, Mum!' she replied, 'the honeymoon was so wonderful and romantic...' But then suddenly she burst out crying and said, 'But, Mum, as soon as we returned home, he started using the most horrible language... things I'd never heard before! I mean, all those awful four-letter words! You've got to come and take me home. Please, Mum!'

'Darling, darling,' her mother said, 'calm down and tell me, what words could be so awful?'

And the daughter cried, 'Please don't make me tell you, Mum! I'm so embarrassed – they're just too awful! Just come and get me, please!'

'Oh, darling, you must tell me what has you so upset... tell me these horrible four-letter words!'

Still sobbing, the bride said, 'Oh, Mum... words like *dust, wash, iron, cook...!*'

Honour

Johnny Lingo lived in the South Pacific. The islanders all spoke highly of this man, but when it came time for him to find a wife, the people shook their heads in disbelief. In order to obtain a wife, you paid for her by giving her father cows. Four to six cows was considered a high price. But the woman Johnny Lingo chose was plain, skinny and walked with her shoulders hunched and her head down. She was very hesitant and shy. What surprised everyone was Johnny's offer – he gave eight cows for her! Everyone chuckled about it, since they believed his father-in-law had put one over on him.

Several months after the wedding, a visitor from the US came to the islands to trade and heard the story about Johnny Lingo and his eight-cow wife. Upon meeting Johnny and his wife, the visitor was astonished, since this wasn't a shy, plain and hesitant woman but one who was beautiful, poised and confident.

The visitor asked about the transformation, and Johnny Lingo's response was very simple. 'I wanted an eight-cow woman, and when I paid that for her and treated her in that fashion, she began to believe that she was an eight-cow woman. She discovered she was worth more than any other woman in the islands. And what matters most is what a woman thinks about herself.'

If a man wants his wife to treat him like a King, then he had better start treating her like a Queen.

Anon

"YOUR coat, Norman, NOT mine."

Husbands

Husbands, love your wives, just as Christ loved the church and gave himself up for her to make her holy, cleansing her by the washing with water through the word, and to present her to himself as a radiant church, without stain or wrinkle or any other blemish, but holy and blameless. In this same way, husbands ought to love their wives as their own bodies. He who loves his wife loves himself. After all, no one ever hated his own body, but he feeds and cares for it, just as Christ does the church – for we are members of his body. 'For this reason a man will leave his father and mother and be united to his wife, and the two will become one flesh.' This is a profound mystery – but I am talking about Christ and the church. However, each one of you also must love his wife as he loves himself, and the wife must respect her husband.

Ephesians 5:25–33, NIV

A husband is a man who after emptying the ashtray, manages to look as if he had just finished cleaning the whole house.

James Simpson

Some helpful hints for a husband who wants to see his spouse experience God's best are posted in *Daddy's Home* by Greg Johnson and Mike Yorkey. A husband can:

- Back off (give her some space).
- Be patient (don't rush things).
- Love her as you love your own body (that's going to take some work).
- Affirm her role in the family (whether she stays home or works outside the home, she's got the most important job in the world).
- Pray for her as you've never prayed before (because God hears our prayers).
- Lower your expectations (you're not going to see fireworks every night).

- Do the little things (without expecting anything in return).
- Show her she's the most cherished woman on earth (she'll probably faint the first time you do this).
- Above all, persevere (you're in this for the long haul).
- A wise husband builds his mate's self-esteem, realizing that the subtle words and actions of a sinful world constantly assault her sense of self-worth. He remains sensitive to her needs and is always ready to offer his support.
- Encourage your wife verbally and demonstratively. Words of cheer and praise are high-octane fuel that boost your wife's emotional fuel tanks.

A husband shopping centre was opened, where a woman could choose a husband from among many men.

It was laid out on five floors, with the men increasing in positive attributes as you ascended the floors. The only rules were that once you opened the door to any floor, you must choose a man from that floor. And if you went up a floor, you couldn't go back down, except to leave the place.

So, a couple of girlfriends go to the shopping centre to find a husband.

First floor: The door has a sign saying, 'These men have jobs and love kids.'

The women read the sign and say, 'Well, that's better than not having jobs or not loving kids, but let's see what's further up.'

And up they go.

Second floor: 'These men have high-paying jobs, love kids and are extremely good looking.'

'Hmmm,' say the girls. 'But what's further up?'

Third floor: 'These men have high-paying jobs, are extremely good looking, love kids, and help with the housework.'

'Wow!' say the women. 'Very tempting. But there's more further up!'

And so again, up they go.

Fourth floor: 'These men have high-paying jobs, love kids, are extremely good looking, help with the housework and have a strong romantic streak.'

'Oh, mercy me!' they exclaim. 'But just think what must be awaiting us further on!'

So, up to the fifth floor they go. The sign on the door says: 'This is just to prove that women are impossible to please. Thank you for shopping, and have a nice day.'

Men are horribly tedious when they are good husbands, and abominably conceited when they are not.

Oscar Wilde

A diplomatic husband said to his wife, 'How do you expect me to remember your birthday when you never look any older?'

Husbands are like fires. They go out if unattended.

Zsa Zsa Gabor

Never trust a husband too far, nor a bachelor too near.

Helen Rowland

It is an easier thing to be a lover than a husband, for the same reason that it is more difficult to be witty every day than now and then.

Balzac

Joseph H. Choate was a thorough gentleman as well as a distinguished lawyer in this country some years back. He had a quick wit, which made him good copy for journalists.

Someone once asked him, 'Mr Choate, if you were not yourself, who would you most like to be?'

Without a second's hesitation Choate replied, 'Mrs Choate's second husband.'

The following is from an actual 1950s home economics textbook intended for high-school girls, teaching them how to prepare for married life:

1. Have dinner ready. Plan ahead, even the night before, to have a delicious meal – on time. This is a way of letting him know that you have been thinking about him and are concerned about his needs. Most men are hungry when they come home and the prospects of a good meal are part of the warm welcome needed.

2. Prepare yourself. Take 15 minutes to rest so you will be refreshed when he arrives. Touch up your make-up, put a ribbon in your hair and be fresh looking. He has just been with a lot of work-weary people. Be a little gay and a little more interesting. His boring day may need a lift.

3. Clear away clutter. Make one last trip through the main part of the house just before your husband arrives, gathering up school books, toys, paper, etc. Then run a dust cloth over the tables. Your husband will feel he has reached a haven of rest and order, and it will give you a lift too.

4. Prepare the children. Take a few minutes to wash the children's hands and faces if they are small, comb their hair, and if necessary, change their clothes. They are little treasures and he would like to see them playing the part.

5. Minimize the noise. At the time of his arrival, eliminate all noise of washer, dryer, or vacuum. Try to encourage the children to be quiet. Greet him with a warm smile and be glad to see him.

6. Some DONT'S. Don't greet him with problems or complaints. Don't complain if he's late for dinner. Count this as minor compared with what he might have gone through that day.

7. Make him comfortable. Have him lean back in a comfortable chair or suggest he lay down in the bedroom. Have a cool or warm drink ready for him. Arrange his pillow and offer to take off his shoes. Speak in a low, soft, soothing and pleasant voice. Allow him to relax and unwind.

8. Listen to him. You may have a dozen things to tell him, but the moment of his arrival is not the time. Let him talk first.

9. Make the evening his. Never complain if he does not take you out to dinner or to other places of entertainment; instead try to understand his world of strain and pressure and his need to be home and relax.

10. The Goal. Try to make your home a place of peace and order where your husband can relax.

In-laws

Q. What's the difference between in-laws and outlaws?
A. Outlaws are wanted!

Intimacy

After just a few years of marriage filled with constant arguments, a young man and his wife decided the only way to save their marriage was to try counselling. They had been at each other's throats for some time and felt that this was their last straw.

When they arrived at the counsellor's office, the counsellor jumped right in and opened the floor for discussion: 'What seems to be the problem?'

Immediately, the husband held his long face down without anything to say. In contrast, the wife began talking at ninety miles an hour, describing all the wrongs within their marriage.

After fifteen minutes of listening to the wife, the counsellor went over to her and gave her a long and lingering kiss on the mouth. Then he went and sat back down.

Afterwards, the wife sat speechless. The counsellor looked over at the husband, who stared in disbelief. The counsellor said to the husband, 'Your wife *needs* that at least twice a week!'

The husband scratched his head and replied, 'I can have her here on Tuesdays and Thursdays.'

Jesus

On the third day a wedding took place at Cana in Galilee. Jesus' mother was there, and Jesus and his disciples had also been invited to the wedding. When the wine was gone, Jesus' mother said to him, 'They have no more wine.'

'Dear woman, why do you involve me?' Jesus replied. 'My time has not yet come.'

His mother said to the servants, 'Do whatever he tells you.'

Nearby stood six stone water jars, the kind used by the Jews for ceremonial washing, each holding from twenty to thirty gallons.

Jesus said to the servants, 'Fill the jars with water'; so they filled them to the brim.

Then he told them, 'Now draw some out and take it to the master of the banquet.'

They did so, and the master of the banquet tasted the water that had been turned into wine. He did not realize where it had come from, though the servants who had drawn the water knew.

Then he called the bridegroom aside and said, 'Everyone brings out the choice wine first and then the cheaper wine after the guests have had too much to drink; but you have saved the best till now.'

This, the first of his miraculous signs, Jesus performed at Cana in Galilee. He thus revealed his glory, and his disciples put their faith in him.

John 2:1–11, NIV

Jewellery

I think men who have a pierced ear are better prepared for marriage. They've experienced pain and bought jewellery.

Rita Rudner

There was a woman who had an artist paint a portrait of her covered with the most amazingly beautiful and expensive jewels.

Her explanation: 'If I die and my husband remarries, I want his next wife to go crazy looking for the jewels.'

Journey

Motto for the bride and groom:
We are a work in progress with a lifetime contract.

Phyllis Koss

You don't marry one person; you marry three: the person you think they are, the person they are, and the person they are going to become as a result of being married to you.

Richard Needham

"He does...er. I do, um, we will...so help me God."

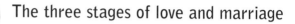

The three stages of love and marriage

1. You don't know 'em, but you love 'em.
2. You know 'em, and don't love 'em.
3. You know 'em and you love 'em.

Anon

The bonds of matrimony are like any other bonds – they mature slowly.

Peter De Vries

Justice

Live so that when your children think of fairness, caring and integrity, they think of you.

H. Jackson Brown, Jr

The right to marry whoever one wishes is an elementary human right compared to which 'the right to attend an integrated school, the right to sit where one pleases on a bus, the right to go into any hotel or recreation area or place of amusement, regardless of one's skin or color or race' are minor indeed. Even political rights, like the right to vote, and nearly all other rights enumerated in the Constitution, are secondary to the inalienable human rights to 'life, liberty and the pursuit of happiness' proclaimed in the Declaration of Independence; and to this category the right to home and marriage unquestionably belongs.

Hannah Arendt

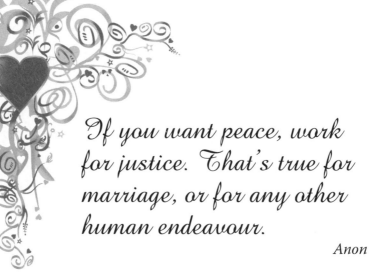

If you want peace, work for justice. That's true for marriage, or for any other human endeavour.

Anon

Kids

A kids' view of marriage

1. What exactly is marriage?
- Marriage is when you get to keep your girl and don't have to give her back to her parents. *(Eric, six years old)*
- When somebody's been dating for a while, the boy might propose to the girl. He says to her, 'I'll take you for a whole life, or at least until we have kids and get divorced, but you've got to do one particular thing for me.' Then she says yes, but she's wondering what the thing is and whether it's naughty or not. She can't wait to find out. *(Anita, nine years old)*

2. How does a person decide whom to marry?
- You flip a coin, and heads means you stay with him and tails means you try the next one. *(Kelly, nine years old)*
- My mother says to look for a man who is kind... That's what I'll do... I'll find somebody who's kinda tall and handsome. *(Carolyn, eight years old)*

3. Concerning the proper age to get married
- Once I'm done with kindergarten, I'm going to find me a wife. *(Bert, five years old)*

4. How did your mum and dad meet?
- They were at a dance party at a friend's house. Then they went for a drive, but their car broke down... It was a good thing, because it gave them a chance to find out about their values. *(Lottie, nine years old)*
- My father was doing some strange chores for my mother. They won't tell me what kind. *(Jeremy, eight years old)*

5. What do most people do on a date?

- On the first date, they just tell each other lies, and that usually gets them interested enough to go for a second date. *(Martin, ten years old)*
- Many daters just eat pork chops and French fries and talk about love. *(Craig, nine years old)*

6. When is it OK to kiss someone?

- You should never kiss a girl unless you have enough bucks to buy her a ring and her own VCR, 'cause she'll want to have videos of the wedding.' *(Allan, ten years old)*
- Never kiss in front of other people. It's a big embarrassing thing if anybody sees you... If nobody sees you, I might be willing to try it with a handsome boy, but just for a few hours. *(Kally, nine years old)*

7. The Great Debate: Is it better to be single or married?

- You should ask the people who read Cosmopolitan. *(Kirsten, ten years old)*
- It's better for girls to be single but not for boys. Boys need somebody to clean up after them. *(Anita, nine years old)*
- It gives me a headache to think about that stuff. I'm just a kid. I don't need that kind of trouble. *(Will, seven years old)*

Kindness

A woman accompanied her husband to the doctor's office. After his check-up, the doctor called the wife into his office alone.

He said, 'Your husband is suffering from a very serious disease, combined with horrible stress. If you don't do the following, your husband can die. Each morning, fix him a healthy breakfast. Be pleasant and make sure he is in a good mood. For lunch, fix him a nutritious meal. For dinner, prepare an especially nice meal for him. Don't burden him with chores. Don't discuss your stress; this will probably make him feel worse.

If you can do this for at least ten months to a year, I think your husband will regain his health completely.'

On the way home, the husband asked his wife, 'What did the doctor say to you?'

'You're going to die.'

Kissing

In colonial days, a Boston sea captain named Kemble was sentenced to spend two hours in the stocks for kissing his wife in public on Sunday, the day he returned from three years at sea.

At the end of their first date, a young man takes his favourite girl home. Emboldened by the night, he decides to try for that important first kiss. With an air of confidence, he leans with his hand against the wall and, smiling, he says to her, 'Darling, how about a goodnight kiss?'

Horrified, she replies, 'Are you mad? My parents will see us!'

'Oh, come on! Who's gonna see us at this hour?'

'No, please. Can you imagine if we get caught?'

'Oh, come on, there's nobody around – they're all sleeping!'

'No way. It's just too risky!'

'Oh, please, please – I like you so much!'

'No, no, and no. I like you too, but I just can't!'

'Oh yes you can. Please?'

'No, no! I just can't.'

'Pleeeeease…?'

Just then, the porch light goes on, and the girl's sister shows up in her pyjamas, hair dishevelled, and says in a sleepy voice:

'Dad says to go ahead and give him a kiss. Or I can do it. Or if need be, he'll come down himself and do it. But for goodness' sake tell him to take his hand off the intercom button!'

Professors of different subjects define the word 'kiss' in different ways:

- A Professor of Computer Science: 'A kiss is a few bits of love compiled into a byte.'
- A Professor of Algebra: 'A kiss is two divided by nothing.'
- A Professor of Geometry: 'A kiss is the shortest distance between two straight lines.'
- A Professor of Physics: 'A kiss is the contraction of mouth due to the expansion of the heart.'
- A Professor of Chemistry: 'A kiss is the reaction to the interaction between two hearts.'
- A Professor of Zoology: 'A kiss is the interchange of unisexual salivary bacteria.'
- A Professor of Physiology: 'A kiss is the juxtaposition of two orbicular ors muscles in the state of contraction.'

- A Professor of Dentistry: 'A kiss is infectious and antiseptic.'
- A Professor of Accountancy: 'A kiss is a credit because it is profitable when returned.'
- A Professor of Economics: 'A kiss is that thing for which the demand is higher than the supply.'
- A Professor of Statistics: 'A kiss is an event whose probability depends on the vital statistics of 36–24–36.'
- A Professor of Philosophy: 'A kiss is persecution for the child, ecstasy for the youth and homage for the old.'
- A Professor of English: 'A kiss is a noun that is used as a conjunction; it is more common than proper; it is spoken in the plural and it is applicable to all.'
- A Professor of Engineering: 'Uh, What? I'm not familiar with that term.'

A kiss is an operation,
cunningly devised, for the
mutual stoppage of speech at
a moment when words are
utterly superfluous.

Anon

Some insurance companies and psychologists have found a correlation between work attitudes and a morning goodbye kiss. Studies show that men who do not kiss their wives goodbye are apt to be moody, depressed and uninterested in their jobs. But kissing husbands start off the day on a positive note. This positive attitude results in more efficient and safer driving practices. Kissing husbands live five years longer than their less romantic counterparts. However, kissing may be more a consequence than a cause of a happy life situation. The subject warrants continued investigation by every husband and wife.

After five years of exhaustive laboratory study sponsored by the United States Public Health Service, Dr Doran D. Zimmer of Daytona, Florida, concluded that kissing can cause tooth decay.

There is one couple I shall always remember from my days as a hospital admitting clerk. The husband, a heart-attack victim, was immediately whisked away by the staff. Hours passed, though, before his wife was allowed to see him. She was dismayed to find him hooked up to elaborate machines that blipped, hissed and beeped.

She tiptoed toward his bed and, bending over him, whispered, 'George, I'm here.' Then she kissed him. Suddenly there was a blippety-blip-blip from the equipment.

'He was OK,' she later explained. 'But after forty-seven years of marriage it's nice to know that I can still make his heart skip when I kiss him.'

Katie Barnes

Before I heard the doctors tell the dangers of a kiss,
I had considered kissing you the nearest thing to bliss.
But now I know biology and sit and sigh and moan;
Six million mad bacteria, and I thought we were alone.

Anon

Laughter

Sexiness wears thin after a while, and beauty fades. But to be married to a man who makes you laugh every day, ah, now that's a real treat.

Joanne Woodward

Laughter is an instant vacation.

Milton Berle

A keen sense of humour helps us to overlook the unbecoming, understand the unconventional, tolerate the unpleasant, overcome the unexpected, and outlast the unbearable.
Billy Graham

Every survival kit should include a sense of humour.

Anon

A laugh is a smile that bursts.

Mary H. Waldrip

Everyone laughs in the same language.

Anon

"I've only ever seen them on the satellite channels. They're even funnier live!"

The human race has only one really effective weapon and that is laughter.

Mark Twain

We are all here for a spell;
get all the good laughs you can.

Will Rogers

Letters

The American poet Anne Bradstreet emigrated with her husband to America in 1630. He was a magistrate for the Massachusetts colony, and spent long periods away from home. Anne missed him terribly, and wrote many love poems to him while he was away, including 'To My Dear and Loving Husband' (1678). She wrote:

> If ever two were one then surely we.
> If ever man were loved by wife, then thee.
> If ever wife were happy in a man,
> Compare with me, ye women, if you can.
> I prize thy love more than whole mines of gold
> Or all the riches that the East doth hold.
> My love is such that rivers cannot quench
> Nor ought but love from thee, give recompense.

Life

On the first day, God created the dog and said: 'Sit all day by the door of your house and bark at anyone who comes in or walks past. For this, I will give you a lifespan of twenty years.'

The dog said: 'That's a long time to be barking. How about only ten years and I'll give you back the other ten?'

So God agreed.

On the second day, God created the monkey and said: 'Entertain people, do tricks, and make them laugh. For this, I'll give you a twenty-year lifespan.'

The monkey said: 'Monkey tricks for twenty years? That's a pretty long time to perform. How about I give you back ten like the dog did?'

And God agreed.

On the third day, God created the cow and said: 'You must go into the field with the farmer all day long and suffer under the sun, have calves and give milk to support the farmer's family. For this, I will give you a lifespan of sixty years.'

The cow said: 'That's kind of a tough life you want me to live for sixty years. How about twenty and I'll give back the other forty?'

And God agreed again.

On the fourth day, God created man and said: 'Eat, sleep, play, marry and enjoy your life. For this, I'll give you twenty years.'

But man said: 'Only twenty years? Could you possibly give me my twenty, the forty the cow gave back, the ten the monkey gave back, and the ten the dog gave back; that makes eighty, OK?'

'OK,' said God, 'you asked for it.'

So that is why for the first twenty years we eat, sleep, play and enjoy ourselves. For the next forty years we slave in the sun to support our family. For the next ten years we do monkey tricks to entertain the grandchildren. And for the last ten years we sit on the front porch and bark at everyone.

Life has now been explained to you.

Listening

My wife says I never listen to her. At least I think that's what she said.

Anon

A couple are reading the paper. The wife says: 'This article on over-population of the world says that somewhere in the world there is a woman having a baby every four seconds!'

Her husband, not wishing to appear uninterested, says: 'I think they ought to find that woman and stop her!'

A husband read an article to his wife about how many words women use in a day – 30,000 to a man's 15,000 words.

The wife replied, 'The reason has to be because a woman has to say everything twice.'

The husband then turned to his wife and asked, 'What?'

Good listening is like tuning in a radio station. For good results, you can listen to only one station at a time. Trying to listen to my wife while looking over an office report is like trying to receive two radio stations at the same time. I end up with distortion and frustration. Listening requires a choice of where I place my attention. To tune into my partner, I must first choose to put away all that will divide my attention. That might mean laying down the newspaper, moving away from the dishes in the sink, putting down the book I'm reading, setting aside my projects.

Robert W. Herron

The first duty of love is to listen.

Paul Tillich

Little things

In the art of marriage, the little things are big things...

- It's never being too old to hold hands.
- It's remembering to say 'I love you' at least once each day.
- It's never going to sleep angry.
- It's having a mutual sense of values and common objectives.
- It's standing together, facing the world.
- It's forming a circle of love that gathers in the whole family.
- It's speaking words of appreciation and demonstrating gratitude in thoughtful ways.
- It's having the capacity to forgive and forget.
- It's giving each other an atmosphere in which each can grow.
- It's a common search for the good and the beautiful.
- It's not only marrying the right partner, but also being the right partner.

Loneliness

I've felt incredible loneliness in my life. I've known great despair. And what is the point of having a great job or something spectacular happening if you have no one to share it with? Unless you have someone, it's pointless. It's vapour.

Julia Roberts

All the money and all the fame in the world is worth nothing if you're lonely.
Tom Cruise

For most people, a life lived alone, with passing strangers or passing lovers, is incoherent and ultimately unbearable. Someone must be there to know what we have done for those we love.
Frank Pittman

A man without a wife is like a vase without flowers.

African proverb

Longevity

Love at first sight is easy to understand; it's when two people have been looking at each other for a lifetime that it becomes a miracle.

Amy Bloom

Some people ask the secret of Anthony's long marriage.

They take time to go to a restaurant two times a week: a little candlelit dinner, soft music, and a slow walk home.

The Mrs goes Tuesdays; he goes Fridays.

Love

Love is what you've been through with somebody.

James Thurber

Love is no assignment for cowards.

Ovid

'What does love mean?' A group of professionals posed this question to a group of four- to eight-year-olds. The answers they got were broader and deeper than anyone could have imagined:

- When my grandmother got arthritis, she couldn't bend over and paint her toenails any more. So my grandfather does it for her all the time, even when his hands got arthritis too. That's love. (Rebecca, age eight)
- When someone loves you, the way they say your name is different. You just know that your name is safe in their mouth. (Billy, age four)
- Love is when a girl puts on perfume and a boy puts on shaving cologne and they go out and smell each other. (Karl, age five)
- Love is when you go out to eat and give somebody most of your French fries without making them give you any of theirs. (Chrissy, age six)
- Love is what makes you smile when you're tired. (Terri, age four)
- Love is when my mum makes coffee for my dad and she takes a sip before giving it to him, to make sure the taste is OK. (Danny, age seven)
- Love is when you kiss all the time. Then when you get tired of kissing, you still want to be together and you talk more. My Mummy and Daddy are like that. They look gross when they kiss. (Emily, age eight)
- Love is what's in the room with you at Christmas if you stop opening presents and listen. (Bobby, age seven)
- If you want to learn to love better, you should start with a friend who you hate. (Nikka, age six) (We need a few million more Nikkas on this planet!)
- Love is when you tell a guy you like his shirt, then he wears it every day. (Noelle, age seven)
- Love is like a little old woman and a little old man who are still friends even after they know each other so well. (Tommy, age six)
- During my piano recital, I was on a stage and I was scared. I looked at all the people watching me and saw my daddy waving and smiling. He was the only one doing that. I wasn't scared any more. (Cindy, age eight)
- My mummy loves me more than anybody. You don't see anyone else kissing me to sleep at night. (Clare, age six)
- Love is when Mummy gives Daddy the best piece of chicken. (Elaine, age five)
- Love is when Mummy sees Daddy smelly and sweaty and still says he is handsomer than Robert Redford. (Chris, age seven)
- Love is when your puppy licks your face even after you left him alone all day. (Mary Ann, age four)
- I know my older sister loves me because she gives me all her old clothes and has to go out and buy new ones. (Lauren, age four)
- When you love somebody, your eyelashes go up and down and little stars come out of you. (Karen, age seven) (What an imagination!)
- Love is when Mummy sees Daddy on the toilet and she doesn't think it's gross. (Mark, age six)
- You really shouldn't say 'I love you' unless you mean it. But if you mean it, you should say it a lot. People forget. (Jessica, age eight)

"When he's mastered this trick, I'll see if I can get him to
scratch behind his ear with his leg."

If I speak in the tongues of men and of angels, but have not love, I am only a resounding gong or a clanging cymbal. If I have the gift of prophecy and can fathom all mysteries and all knowledge, and if I have a faith that can move mountains, but have not love, I am nothing. If I give all I possess to the poor and surrender my body to the flames, but have not love, I gain nothing.

Love is patient, love is kind. It does not envy, it does not boast, it is not proud. It is not rude, it is not self-seeking, it is not easily angered, it keeps no record of wrongs. Love does not delight in evil but rejoices with the truth. It always protects, always trusts, always hopes, always perseveres.

Love never fails. But where there are prophecies, they will cease; where there are tongues, they will be stilled; where there is knowledge, it will pass away. For we know in part and we prophesy in part, but when perfection comes, the imperfect disappears.

When I was a child, I talked like a child, I thought like a child, I reasoned like a child. When I became a man, I put childish ways behind me. Now we see but a poor reflection as in a mirror; then we shall see face to face. Now I know in part; then I shall know fully, even as I am fully known.

And now these three remain: faith, hope and love. But the greatest of these is love.

1 Corinthians 13, NIV

One member of a couple says (as if this is an excuse for leaving), 'I love him (or her), but I am no longer in love.' Love is an action word, I want to say. When was the last time you 'loved' him (or her) by your actions? Love is not just a feeling. Love is a verb.

Riette Smith

Dr Robert Seizer, in his book *Mortal Lessons: Notes in the Art of Surgery*, tells a remarkable story of performing surgery to remove a tumour in which it was necessary to sever a facial nerve, leaving a young woman's mouth permanently twisted in palsy. In Dr Seizer's own words:

> Her young husband is in the room. He stands on the opposite side of the bed, and together they seem to dwell in the evening lamp light, isolated from me, private. Who are they, I ask myself, he and this wry-mouth I have made, who gaze at and touch each other so generously, greedily? The young woman speaks. 'Will my mouth always be like this?' she asks. 'Yes,' I say, 'it will. It is because the nerve was cut.' She nods, and is silent. But the young man smiles. 'I like it,' he says. 'It is kind of cute.' All at once I know who he is. I understand, and I lower my gaze. One is not bold in an encounter with God. Unmindful, he bends to kiss her crooked mouth, and I, so close, can see how he twists his own lips to accommodate to hers, to show her that their kiss still works.

Love is not breathlessness, it is not excitement, it is not promises of eternal passion, it is not the desire to mate every second minute of the day, it is not lying awake at night imagining that he is kissing every cranny of your body. No, don't blush. I am telling you some truths. That is just being 'in love,' which any fool can do. Love itself is what is left over when being in love has burned away... Your mother and I had it, we had roots that grew towards each other underground, and when all the pretty blossoms had fallen from the branches, we found that we were one tree and not two.

A widowed father to his daughter in the novel
Captain Corelli's Mandolin, *Louis De Bernières (1994)*

Marriage

Marriage should be honoured by all, and the marriage bed kept pure, for God will judge the adulterer and all the sexually immoral.

Hebrews 13:4, NIV

Marriage is a gift of God in creation through which husband and wife may know the grace of God. It is given that as man and woman grow together in love and trust, they shall be united with one another in heart, body and mind, as Christ is united with his bride, the Church.

The gift of marriage brings husband and wife together in the delight and tenderness of sexual union and joyful commitment to the end of their lives. It is given as the foundation of family life in which children are [born and] nurtured and in which each member of the family, in good times and in bad, may find strength, companionship and comfort, and grow to maturity in love.

Marriage is a way of life made holy by God, and blessed by the presence of our Lord Jesus Christ with those celebrating a wedding at Cana in Galilee. Marriage is a sign of unity and loyalty which all should uphold and honour. It enriches society and strengthens community. No one should enter into it lightly or selfishly but reverently and responsibly in the sight of almighty God.

From the Wedding Service in Common Worship

There is nothing more admirable than two people who see eye to eye keeping house as man and wife, confounding their enemies, and delighting their friends.

Homer

Marriage is love. Love is blind. Marriage is an institution. Therefore, marriage is an institution for the blind.

Anon

Marriage is a lot like the army: everyone complains, but you'd be surprised at the large number that re-enlist.

James Garner

There is no such cosy combination as man and wife.

Menander

I told someone I was getting married, and they said, 'Have you picked a date yet?'

I said, 'Wow, you can bring a date to your own wedding?' What a country!

Yakov Smirnoff

The secret to having a good marriage is to understand that marriage must be total, it must be permanent, and it must be equal.

Frank Pittman

The first bond
of society is
marriage.

Cicero

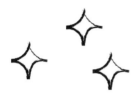

Matrimony:
The high sea for which
no compass has yet
been invented.

Anon

Marriage is not
a word. It is a
sentence. A life
sentence.

Anon

By all means marry! If you get a good wife, you'll be happy. If you get a bad one, you'll become a philosopher.

Socrates

Marriage is very much like a violin; after the sweet music is over the strings are attached.

Anon

It is not your love that sustains the marriage, but from now on, the marriage that sustains your love.

Dietrich Bonhoeffer, writing to a young bride and groom from his prison cell in Nazi Germany in 1943

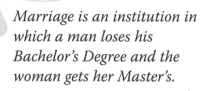

Marriage is an institution in which a man loses his Bachelor's Degree and the woman gets her Master's.

Anon

The happy State of Matrimony is, undoubtedly, the surest and most lasting Foundation of Comfort and Love... the Cause of all good Order in the World, and what alone preserves it from the utmost Confusion...

Benjamin Franklin

Marriage is a thing which puts a ring on a woman's finger... and two under the man's eyes.

Anon

A man is not complete until he is married — then he is finished.

Anon

A husband is living proof that a wife can take a joke.

Anon

They say marriages are made in Heaven. But so is thunder and lightning.

Clint Eastwood

The most happy marriage I can imagine to myself would be the union of a deaf man to a blind woman.

S. T. Coleridge

Marriage is bliss. Ignorance is bliss. Ergo…

Anon

Married life is very frustrating. In the first year of marriage, the man speaks and the wife listens. In the second year, the woman speaks and the husband listens. In the third year, they both speak and the neighbours listen.

Anon

I think, therefore I am single.

Anon

If variety is the spice of life, marriage is the big can of left-over Spam.

Johnny Carson

An archaeologist is the best husband a woman can have; the older she gets, the more interested he is in her.

Agatha Christie

The trouble with some women is that they get all excited about nothing – and then marry him.

Cher

Marriage is a three-ring circus: engagement ring, wedding ring, and suffering.

Anon

I never knew what real happiness was until I got married and by then, it was too late.

Anon

If you want to sacrifice the admiration of many men for the criticism of one, go ahead, get married.

Katharine Hepburn

Eighty per cent of married men cheat in America. The rest cheat in Europe.

Jackie Mason

Honolulu, it's got everything. Sand for the children, sun for the wife, sharks for the wife's mother.
Ken Dodd

*"It was sweet of you to notice how much Mum needed a break –
this has really revitalised her."*

Maturity

Like good wine, marriage gets better with age – once you learn to keep a cork in it.

Gene Perret

Memory

A couple were invited to dinner by their elderly neighbours. The old gentleman endearingly preceded every request to his wife with 'Honey', 'Darling', 'Sweetheart', 'Pumpkin' and so on. The neighbours were impressed, since the couple had been married almost seventy years.

While the wife was off in the kitchen, the neighbour said to the gentleman, 'I think it's wonderful that after all the years you've been married, you still refer to your wife in those terms.'

The elderly husband hung his head. 'Actually, I forgot her name about ten years ago.'

Marriage is the alliance of two people, one of whom never remembers birthdays and the other who never forgets.

Ogden Nash

Arnold and Betty were cleaning out the attic one day when he came across a ticket from the local shoe-repair shop. The date stamped on the ticket showed it was over eleven years old. They both laughed and tried to remember which of them might have forgotten to pick up a pair of shoes over a decade ago.

'Do you think the shoes will still be in the shop?' Arnold asked.

'Not very likely,' Betty said.

'It's worth a try,' Arnold said, pocketing the ticket.

He went downstairs, hopped into the car, and drove to the store. With a straight face, he handed the ticket to the man behind the counter.

With a face just as straight, the man said, 'Just a minute. I'll have to look for these.'

He disappeared into a dark corner at the back of the shop. Two minutes later, the man called out, 'Here they are!'

'No kidding?' Arnold called back. 'That's terrific! Who would have thought they'd still be here after all this time.'

The man came back to the counter, empty-handed.

'They'll be ready on Thursday,' he said calmly.

*T*wo elderly couples were chatting together. One of the men asked the other, 'Fred, how was the visit to the memory clinic last month?'

'Outstanding. They taught us some of the latest techniques for remembering things. It was great.'

'What was the name of this clinic?' asked the other man.

Fred's mind went blank. Then he smiled and asked, 'What do you call that flower with the long stem and thorns?'

'A rose?'

'Yes!'

He turned to his wife. 'Rose, what was the name of that memory clinic?'

An elderly widow and widower were dating for about five years. The man finally decided to ask her to marry him. She immediately said 'Yes.'

The next morning, when he awoke, he couldn't remember what her answer was! 'Was she happy? I think so... Wait... no, she looked at me funny...'

After about an hour of trying to remember to no avail, he got on the telephone and gave her a call. Embarrassed, he admitted that he didn't remember her answer to the marriage proposal.

'Oh,' she said, 'I'm so glad you called. I remembered saying "Yes" to someone, but I couldn't remember who it was.'

The conductor Sir Thomas Beecham was attending a prestigious reception, and was in conversation with someone he recognized but whose name he could not recall. He began the conversation, desperate to find a clue to the person's identity.

'So are you well?'

'Yes, thank you.'

'And the family?'

'Yes, they are fine.'

'And your husband, is he well?'

'Yes, very well, thank you.'

'And is he still in the same line of business?'

'Yes, he's still King.'

Men

A man is walking down the beach and comes across an old bottle. He picks it up, pulls out the cork, and out pops a genie.

'Thank you for freeing me from the bottle,' says the genie. 'In return I shall grant you three wishes.'

'Great!' says the man. 'I always dreamed of this, and I know exactly what I want. First, I want a billion pounds in a Swiss bank account.'

Poof! There, in a flash of light, is a piece of paper with account numbers on it.

'Second, I want a brand-new red Ferrari right now,' he continues.

Poof! There is a flash of light and a red Ferrari appears, right next to him.

'Third, I want to be irresistible to women.'

Poof! There is a flash of light and he turns into a box of chocolates!

Why men are happier people

- Your last name stays put.
- The garage is all yours.
- Wedding plans take care of themselves.
- Chocolate is just another snack.
- You can be president.
- You can wear a white T-shirt to a water park.
- You can wear *no* T-shirt to a water park.
- Car mechanics tell you the truth.
- The world is your bathroom.
- You never have to drive to another petrol station because 'This one's just too icky.'
- You don't have to stop and think of which way to turn a nut on a bolt.
- Same work, more pay.
- Wrinkles add character.
- Wedding dress – £2,000; tux rental – £100.
- People never stare at your chest when you're talking to them.
- The occasional well-rendered belch is practically expected.
- New shoes don't cut, blister or mangle your feet.
- One mood, *all* the time.
- Phone conversations are over in thirty seconds flat.
- You know stuff about tanks.
- A five-day holiday requires only one suitcase.
- You can open all your own jars.
- You get extra credit for the slightest act of thoughtfulness.
- If someone forgets to invite you, he or she can still be your friend.
- Your underwear is £5.99 for a three-pack.
- Three pairs of shoes are more than enough (one black pair, two sports pairs).
- You almost never have strap problems in public.
- You are unable to see wrinkles in your clothes.
- Everything on your face stays its original colour.
- The same hairstyle lasts for years, maybe decades.
- You only have to shave your face and neck.
- You can play with toys all your life.
- Your belly usually hides your big hips.
- One wallet and one pair of shoes, one colour, all seasons.
- You can wear shorts, no matter how your legs look.
- You can 'do' your nails with a pocket knife.
- You have freedom of choice concerning growing a moustache.
- You can do Christmas shopping for 25 relatives, on Christmas Eve, in 45 minutes.

No wonder men are happier!

We always hear 'the rules' from the female side. Now here are the rules from the male side:

- Learn to work the toilet seat. You're a big girl. If it's up, put it down. We need it up, you need it down. You don't hear us complaining about you leaving it down.
- Weekend = sport. It's like the full moon or the changing of the tides. Let it be.
- Shopping is not a sport. And no, we are never going to think of it that way.
- Crying is blackmail.
- Ask for what you want. Let us be clear on this one: subtle hints do not work! Strong hints do not work! Obvious hints do not work! Just say it!
- 'Yes' and 'No' are perfectly good answers to almost every question.
- Come to us with a problem if you only want help solving it. That's what we do. Sympathy is what your girlfriends are for.
- A headache that lasts for seventeen months is a problem. See a doctor.
- Anything said six months ago is inadmissible in an argument. In fact all comments become null and void after seven days.
- If you think you're fat you probably are. Don't ask us.
- If something we said can be interpreted two ways, and one way makes you sad and angry, we meant the other one.
- You can either ask us to do something or tell us how you want it done. Not both. If you already know best how to do it, just do it yourself.
- Whenever possible, please say what you want to say during commercials.
- Christopher Columbus did not need directions and neither do we.
- All men see in only sixteen colours, like Windows default settings. 'Peach', for example, is a fruit, not a colour. Pumpkin is also a fruit. We have no idea what mauve is.
- If it itches, it will be scratched. We do that.
- If we ask you what is wrong and you say 'Nothing', we will act like nothing's wrong. We know you are lying, but it's not worth the hassle.
- If you ask a question you don't want the answer to, expect an answer you don't want to hear.
- When we have to go somewhere, absolutely anything you wear will be fine... Really!
- Don't ask us what we're thinking about unless you are prepared to discuss such topics as the offside rule, refereeing decisions, or off-roading.
- You have enough clothes.
- You have too many shoes.
- I am in shape. Round is a shape.

Thank you for reading this. Yes, I know, I have to sleep on the couch tonight. But did you know that men really don't mind? It's like camping.

The top ten things that men understand about women

1.
2.
3.
4.
5.
6.
7.
8.
9.
10.

An English professor wrote the words, 'A woman without her man is nothing' on the blackboard, and directed the students to punctuate it correctly.

The men wrote: 'A woman, without her man, is nothing.'

The women wrote: 'A woman: without her, man is nothing.'

Punctuation is everything.

Men and women

In January 1992, at 1 a.m., one very tired mum heard a cough. I bolted from my sleep to a standing/running position and in one leap made it to the bathroom and flipped on the light to find my 6-year-old daughter sitting on the edge of the bath. The stuff from her tummy was all over the floor, the lid of the toilet, and herself.

I proceeded to clean the floor and surrounding areas, then placed Sarah into the bath to wash down. As I turned on the shower, Sarah said, 'Mum,' with a wrinkled nose and a hesitant voice, 'I threw up on Collett too.'

Collett is her 9-year-old sister, who happens to share the bed. I closed the curtain and ran to see. I met Collett in the hallway, and she said Sarah had thrown up on her. I turned on the bedroom light and much to my amazement, there was the dreaded sight of Sarah's dinner on five blankets, two pillows, two sheets, a baby blanket, and Collett's pyjamas.

I bundled it all up into the bottom sheet and placed it at the back door. I put fresh bedding on the bed and placed a bucket beside Sarah, then I crawled back in my own bed.

At which time, my well-covered, half-asleep husband inquired, 'What's wrong?'

Focus on the Family Newsletter

What Women Want: To be loved, to be listened to, to be desired, to be respected, to be needed, to be trusted, and sometimes, just to be held.

What Men Want: Tickets to a football match.

Dave Barry

A man was sick and tired of going to work every day while his wife stayed home. He wanted her to see what he went through, so he prayed:

'Dear Lord, I go to work every day and put in eight hours while my wife merely stays at home. I want her to know what I go through. So, please allow her body to switch with mine for a day. Amen!'

God, in his infinite wisdom, granted the man's wish. The next morning, sure enough, the man awoke as a woman. He arose, cooked breakfast for his mate, awakened the kids, set out their school clothes, fed them breakfast, packed their lunches, drove them to school, came home and picked up the dry cleaning, took it to the cleaners, and stopped at the bank to make a deposit, went grocery shopping, then drove home to put away the groceries, paid the bills and balanced the cheque book.

He cleaned the cat's litter-box and bathed the dog. Then it was already 1 p.m. and he hurried to make the beds, do the laundry, vacuum, dust, and sweep and mop the kitchen floor. Ran to the school to pick up the kids and got into an argument with them on the way home. Set out milk and cookies and got the kids organized to do their homework. Then, set up the ironing board and watched TV while he did the ironing. At 4:30 he began peeling potatoes and washing vegetables for salad, breaded the pork chops and snapped fresh beans for supper.

After supper, he cleaned the kitchen, ran the dishwasher, folded laundry, bathed the kids, and put them to bed. At 9 p.m. he was exhausted and, though his daily chores weren't finished, he went to bed where he was expected to make love, which he managed to get through without complaint.

The next morning, he awoke and immediately knelt by the bed and said:

'Lord, I don't know what I was thinking. I was so wrong to envy my wife's being able to stay home all day. Please, please, let us trade back. Amen!'

The Lord, in his infinite wisdom, replied: 'My son, I feel you have learned your lesson and I will be happy to change things back to the way they were. You'll just have to wait nine months, though. You got pregnant last night.'

Although this married couple enjoyed their new fishing boat together, it was the husband who was behind the wheel operating the boat. He was concerned about what might happen in an emergency. So one day out on the lake he said to his wife, 'Please take the wheel, dear. Pretend that I am having a heart attack. You must get the boat safely to shore and dock it.'

So she drove the boat to shore. Later that evening, the wife walked into the living room where her husband was watching television. She sat down next to him, switched the TV channel, and said to him, 'Please go into the kitchen, dear. Pretend I'm having a heart attack and set the table, cook dinner and wash the dishes.'

"I AM pretending, honey. When it's for real I'll use black nail-polish."

Are you tired of the battle between the sexes? Men and women are different. There's no question about it. But instead of focusing on the negative qualities of men and women, why not celebrate the positive qualities? Let's start with the ladies:

- Women are compassionate, and loving, and caring.
- Women cry when they are happy.
- Women are always doing little things to show they care.
- They will stop at nothing to get what they think is best for their children (best school, best prom dress, best dentist).
- Women have the ability to keep smiling when they are so tired they can hardly stand up.
- They know how to turn a simple meal into an occasion.
- Women know how to get the most for their money.
- They know how to comfort a sick friend.
- Women bring joy and laughter to the world.
- They know how to entertain children for hours on end!
- They are honest and loyal.
- Women have a will of iron under that soft exterior.
- They will go the extra mile to help a friend in need.
- Women are easily brought to tears by injustice.
- They know how to make a man feel like a king.
- Women make the world a much happier place to live in.

Now for the men:

- Men are good at moving heavy things and removing spiders.

The man's guide to female English

- We need... = I want...
- It's your decision. = The correct decision should be obvious by now.
- Do what you want. = You'll pay for this later.
- We need to talk. = I need to complain.
- You're so... manly. = You need a shave and you sweat a lot.
- You're certainly attentive tonight! = Is sex all you ever think about?
- I want new curtains = and carpeting and furniture, and wallpaper...
- Hang the picture there. = NO, I mean hang it there.
- I heard a noise. = I noticed you were almost asleep.
- Do you love me? = I'm going to ask for something expensive.
- How much do you love me today? = I did something today you're not going to like.
- I'll be ready in a minute. = Kick off your shoes and find a good game on TV.
- You have to learn to communicate. = Just agree with me.
- Yes. = No.
- No. = No.
- Maybe. = No.
- I'm sorry. = You'll be sorry.
- Do you like this recipe? = It's easy to make so you'd better get used to it.

The woman's guide to male English

- I'm hungry. = I'm hungry.
- I'm sleepy. = I'm sleepy.
- I'm tired. = I'm tired.
- Do you want to go to a movie? = I'd eventually like to have sex with you.
- Can I take you out to dinner? = I'd eventually like to have sex with you.
- Can I call you sometime? = I'd eventually like to have sex with you.
- May I have this dance? = I'd eventually like to have sex with you.
- Nice dress! = Nice cleavage!
- You look tense – let me give you a massage. = I want to fondle you.
- What's wrong? = I don't see why you're making such a big deal out of this.
- What's wrong? = What meaningless, self-inflicted psychological trauma are you going through now?
- What's wrong? = I guess sex is out of the question.
- I'm bored. = Do you want to have sex?
- I love you. = Let's have sex now.
- I love you too. = OK, I said it... We'd better have sex now!
- Yes, I like the way you cut your hair. = I liked it better before.
- Let's talk. = I am trying to impress you by showing that I am a deep person, and maybe then you'd like to have sex with me.

Mum and Dad were watching TV when Mum said, 'I'm tired, and it's getting late. I think I'll go to bed.'

She went to the kitchen to make sandwiches for the next day's lunches, rinsed out the popcorn bowls, took meat out of the freezer for supper the following evening, checked the cereal-box levels, filled the sugar container, put spoons and bowls on the table and started the coffee pot for brewing the next morning. She then put some wet clothes in the dryer, put a load of clothes into the wash, ironed a shirt and secured a loose button. She picked up the game pieces left on the table and put the telephone book back into the drawer.

She watered the plants, emptied a wastebasket and hung up a towel to dry. She yawned and stretched and headed for the bedroom. She stopped by the desk and wrote a note to the teacher, counted out some cash for the field trip, and pulled a textbook out from hiding under the chair. She signed a birthday card for a friend, addressed and stamped the envelope and wrote a quick note for the grocery store. She put both near her purse.

Mum then creamed her face, put on moisturizer, brushed and flossed her teeth and trimmed her nails. Hubby called, 'I thought you were going to bed.'

'I'm on my way,' she said. She put some water into the dog's dish and put the cat outside, then made sure the doors were locked. She looked in on each of the kids and turned off a bedside lamp, hung up a shirt, threw some dirty socks into the laundry basket, and had a brief conversation with one of her children who was still doing homework. In her own room, she set the alarm, laid out clothing for the next day, and straightened up the shoe-rack. She added three things to her list of things to do for tomorrow.

About that time, the hubby turned off the TV and announced to no one in particular, 'I'm going to bed.' And he did.

On a transatlantic flight, a plane passes through a severe storm. The turbulence is awful, and things go from bad to worse when one wing is struck by lightning.

One woman loses it. Screaming, she wails, 'I'm too young to die!'

Then she yells, 'Well, if I'm going to die, I want my last minutes on earth to be memorable! Is there anyone on this plane who can make me feel like a woman?'

For a moment there is silence. Everyone has forgotten their own peril. They all stare at the desperate woman at the front of the plane.

Then a man stands up at the rear of the plane. He is gorgeous – tall, well built, with reddish-blond hair and hazel eyes. He starts to walk slowly up the aisle, unbuttoning his shirt... one button at a time.

No one moves. He removes his shirt. Muscles ripple across his chest.

He whispers: 'Iron this.'

Mess

I'm very neat. My wife is messy – never picks anything up. Doesn't even notice the mess – it's below her radar.

I cured myself from my annoyance with her by imagining that she had died and then asking myself, 'If you could bring her back to life but she'd still be messy, leave clutter all over the house – five pairs of shoes in the living room, would you still want her back?'

'Yes, for sure!'

And, it cured me. Whenever I get annoyed with her mess, I rerun the script.

Sam Bradley

Money

 A little kid asks his dad, 'Daddy, how much does it cost to get married?'
'No idea,' replies the father. 'I'm still paying for it...'

The cost of marriage puts it beyond the reach of many young people, yet it is the aspiration of an overwhelming majority, according to a survey.

An Ipsos MORI poll of people aged between 20 and 35, done for the right-of-centre Civitas think-tank found that seven in ten wanted to marry. Of those cohabiting, eight out of ten wanted to wed. The most frequently found reason for wanting to marry was to indicate commitment, another large proportion saying that the institution provided a stable environment to bring up children.

The main reason for not having yet married was having not met the right person, but almost a quarter of those surveyed said it was financial: either they could not afford the wedding or were waiting for things to improve, for instance so that they could buy a home. Among cohabiting couples, the number of people giving financial reasons for not having married rose from 24 per cent to 30 per cent. In 2006 the marriage rate was 22.8 per cent, the lowest since records began in 1862.

Anastasia de Waal, author of the report, said: 'In the past, people had to marry – but today, people want to. The last Census and the Millennium Cohort Study reveal that marriage is out of reach for many.'

The Times, *19 May 2008*

A woman was telling her friend, 'It was I who made my husband a millionaire.'

'And what was he before you married him?' asked the friend.

The woman replied, 'A multi-millionaire.'

A teacher was giving her pupils a lesson in logic.

'Here is the situation,' she said. 'A man is standing up in a boat in the middle of a river, fishing. He loses his balance, falls in, and begins splashing and yelling for help. His wife hears the commotion, knows he can't swim, and runs down to the bank. Why do you think she ran to the bank?'

A little girl raised her hand and suggested, 'To draw out all his savings?'

A Sunday School teacher was teaching her class about the difference between right and wrong.

'OK, children, let's take another example,' she said. 'If I were to get into a man's pocket and take his wallet with all his money, what would I be?'

A little boy raised his hand and, with a confident smile, blurted out, 'You'd be his wife!'

Mothers-in-law

A man was travelling down a country road when he saw a large group of people outside a house. He stopped and asked a person why the large crowd was there.

A farmer replied, 'Joe's mule kicked his mother-in-law and she died.'

'Well,' replied the man, 'she must have had a lot of friends.'

'Nope,' said the farmer, 'we all just want to buy his mule.'

A man goes on holiday to the Holy Land with his wife and mother-in-law. The mother-in-law dies.

They go to an undertaker who explains that they can ship the body home, but it'll cost over £5,000, whereas they can bury her in the Holy Land for only £150.

The guy says, 'We'll ship her home.'

The undertaker asks, 'Are you sure? That's an awfully big expense and we can do a very nice burial here.'

The guy says, 'Look, 2,000 years ago they buried a guy here and three days later he rose from the dead. I just can't take that chance.'

Mother-in-law:
a woman who destroys her
son-in-law's peace of mind by
giving him a piece of hers.

Anon

The newly wed wife said to her husband when he returned from work, 'I have great news for you. Pretty soon, we're going to be three in this house instead of two.'

Her husband ran to her with a smile on his face and delight in his eyes.

He was glowing with happiness and kissing his wife when she said, 'I'm glad that you feel this way, since tomorrow morning, my mother moves in with us.'

"Talking of punchlines, Derek."

Mothers

Tony excitedly tells his mother he's fallen in love and is going to get married. He says, 'Just for fun, Mum, I'm going to bring over two other female friends in addition to my fiancée, and you have to guess which one I'm going to marry.'

The next day, Tony brings three beautiful women into the house and sits them down on the couch, and they chat for a while.

He then says, 'OK, Mum. Guess which one I'm going to marry.'

She immediately replies, 'The redhead in the middle.'

'That's amazing! You're right. How did you know?'

His mother folds her arms across her chest and says, 'I don't like her.'

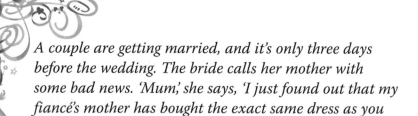

A couple are getting married, and it's only three days before the wedding. The bride calls her mother with some bad news. 'Mum,' she says, 'I just found out that my fiancé's mother has bought the exact same dress as you to wear to the wedding.'

The bride's mother thinks for a minute. 'Don't worry,' she tells her daughter. 'I'll just go and buy another dress to wear to the ceremony.'

'But mother,' says the bride, 'that dress cost a fortune. What will you do with it? It's such a waste not to use it.'

'Who said I won't use it? I'll just wear it to the rehearsal dinner.'

The speaker at a women's club was lecturing on marriage and asked the audience how many of them wanted to 'mother' their husbands.

One member in the back row raised her hand.

'You want to mother your husband?' the speaker asked.

'Mother?' the woman echoed. 'I thought you said *smother*!'

N

Nurture

Marriages may be made
in heaven, but man is
responsible for the
maintenance work.

Anon

One of the great illusions of our time is that love is self-sustaining. It is not. Love must be fed and nurtured, constantly renewed. That demands ingenuity and consideration, but first and foremost, it demands time.

David Mace

Married happiness is like a tree; it has to grow before you can enjoy its shade. And it doesn't grow if you don't take care of it but run around admiring other plants. It takes many years. If you concentrate your love on a single tree and wait, you can see it grow, and there comes a day when you can lean against it and find coolness in its shade.

From The Princess *by Gunnar Mattsson*

A great proportion of the wretchedness which has embittered married life has originated in a negligence of trifles. Connubial happiness is a thing of too fine a texture to be handled roughly. It is a sensitive plant, which will not bear even the touch of unkindness; a delicate flower, which indifference will chill and suspicion blast. It must be watered by showers of tender affections, expanded by the cheering glow of kindness, and guarded by the impregnable barrier of unshaken confidence. Thus matured, it will bloom with fragrance in every season of life, and sweeten even the loneliness of declining years.

Thomas Sprat (1636–1713)

One

The 'one another' verses in the Bible

- *Love* one another – John 13:34; 15:12; 1 Thessalonians 3:12; 4:9; 1 Peter 1:22; 1 John 3:18.
- *Encourage* one another – 1 Thessalonians 4:18; Hebrews 10:24.
- *Spur* one another on (towards love and good deeds) – Hebrews 10:24.
- *Build* one another up – 1 Thessalonians 5:11; Romans 14:19.
- *Admonish* one another – Colossians 3:16.
- *Instruct* one another – Romans 15:14.
- *Serve* one another – Galatians 5:13; 1 Peter 4:10.
- *Bear* with one another – Ephesians 4:32; Colossians 3:13.
- *Forgive* one another – Ephesians 4:32; Colossians 3:13.
- *Be kind* to one another – Ephesians 4:32.
- *Be compassionate* to one another – Ephesians 4:32; 1 Peter 3:8.
- *Be devoted* to one another – Romans 12:10.
- *Honour* one another – Romans 12:10.
- *Live in harmony* with one another – Romans 12:16; 1 Peter 3:8.
- *Be sympathetic* with one another – 1 Peter 3:8.
- *Be patient* with one another – Ephesians 4:2.
- *Accept* one another – Romans 15:7.
- *Submit* to one another – Ephesians 5:21.
- *Clothe yourselves with humility* towards one another – Ephesians 4:2; 1 Peter 5:5.
- *Teach* one another – Colossians 3:16.
- *Live at peace* with one another – Mark 9:50; Romans 12:18.
- *Confess* your sins to one another – James 5:16.
- *Offer hospitality* to one another – 1 Peter 4:9.

Openness

Openness is essentially the willingness to grow, a distaste for ruts, eagerly standing on top-toe for a better view of what tomorrow brings. A man once bought a new radio, brought it home, placed it on the refrigerator, plugged it in, turned it to WSM in Nashville (home of the Grand Ole Opry), and then pulled all the knobs off! He had already tuned in all he ever wanted or expected to hear. Some marriages are 'rutted' and rather dreary because either or both partners have yielded to the tyranny of the inevitable, 'what has been will still be.' Stay open to newness. Stay open to change.

Grady Nutt

Origins

At the beginning of creation God 'made them male and female.' 'For this reason a man will leave his father and mother and be united to his wife, and the two will become one flesh.' So they are no longer two, but one. Therefore what God has joined together, let man not separate.

Mark 10:6–9, NIV

Then God said, 'Let us make man in our image, in our likeness, and let them rule over the fish of the sea and the birds of the air, over the livestock, over all the earth, and over all the creatures that move along the ground.'

> *So God created man in his own image,*
> *in the image of God he created him;*
> *male and female he created them.*

God blessed them and said to them, 'Be fruitful and increase in number; fill the earth and subdue it. Rule over the fish of the sea and the birds of the air and over every living creature that moves on the ground.'

Genesis 1:26–28, NIV

One day in the Garden of Eden, Eve called out to God that she had a problem.

'What's the problem, Eve?' he responded.

'Lord, I know you've created me and have provided this beautiful garden and all of these wonderful animals, but I am still so lonely.'

God replied, 'I have a solution for you, Eve. I shall create a man to keep you company.'

Then Eve inquired, 'What is a "man", Lord?'

God explained, 'A man is a flawed creature with aggressive tendencies, an enormous ego, and an inability to empathize or listen. All in all, he'll make life more difficult, but he will be bigger and more muscular than you, and therefore able to help out around the garden. He'll be really good at fighting and kicking a ball around, and he will enjoy hunting fleet-footed ruminants.'

'OK, if that's the best you can do,' replied Eve.

God chided, 'Yeah, well, he'll be better than a poke in the eye with a burnt stick! Now, you can only have him under one condition.'

'What is it, Lord?' asked Eve.

'You must let him believe that I created him first.'

In the beginning there was Adam...

So God asked him, 'What is wrong with you?'

Adam said he didn't have anyone to talk to. God said that he was going to make Adam a companion and that it would be a woman.

God said, 'This person will gather food for you, cook for you, and when you discover clothing she'll wash it for you. She will always agree with every decision you make. She will bear your children and never ask you to get up in the middle of the night to take care of them. She will not nag you and will always be the first to admit she was wrong when you've had a disagreement. She will never have a headache and will freely give you love and passion whenever you need it.'

Adam asked God, 'What will a woman like this cost?'

God replied, 'An arm and a leg.'

Then Adam asked, 'What can I get for a rib?'

The rest is history.

*T*he Lord God took the man and put him in the Garden of Eden to work it and take care of it. And the Lord God commanded the man, 'You are free to eat from any tree in the garden; but you must not eat from the tree of the knowledge of good and evil, for when you eat of it you will surely die.'

The Lord God said, 'It is not good for the man to be alone. I will make a helper suitable for him.'

Now the Lord God had formed out of the ground all the beasts of the field and all the birds of the air. He brought them to the man to see what he would name them; and whatever the man called each living creature, that was its name. So the man gave names to all the livestock, the birds of the air and all the beasts of the field.

But for Adam no suitable helper was found. So the Lord God caused the man to fall into a deep sleep; and while he was sleeping, he took one of the man's ribs and closed up the place with flesh. Then the Lord God made a woman from the rib he had taken out of the man, and he brought her to the man.

The man said,

This is now bone of my bones
and flesh of my flesh;
she shall be called 'woman',
for she was taken out of man.

For this reason a man will leave his father and mother and be united to his wife, and they will become one flesh.

The man and his wife were both naked, and they felt no shame.

Genesis 2:15–25, NIV

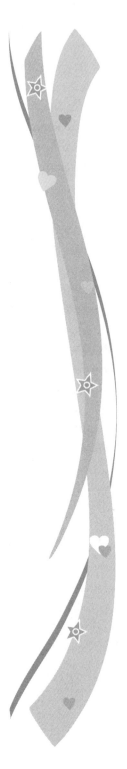

Reasons why God created Eve

1. God was worried that Adam would get lost in the garden and would not ask for directions.
2. God knew that one day Adam would need someone to help him find the remote.
3. God knew Adam would never go out by himself and buy himself a new fig leaf.
4. God knew Adam would never make a doctor's or dentist's appointment on his own.
5. God knew Adam would never remember which night to put out the rubbish.
6. God knew Adam would never handle the responsibility of childbirth.
7. God knew Adam would need help relocating his gardening implements.
8. God knew Adam would need someone else to blame.
9. God finished making Adam, scratched his head and said, 'I can do better than that!'

"I found these in the shed – is Adam seeing someone else?"

Parenting

A couple had two little boys, ages eight and ten, who were excessively mischievous. The two were always getting into trouble, and their parents could be assured that if any mischief occurred in their town, their two young sons were in some way involved. The parents were at their wits' end as to what to do about their sons' behaviour.

The mother had heard that a clergyman in town had been successful in disciplining children in the past, so she asked her husband if he thought they should send the boys to speak with the clergyman.

The husband said, 'We might as well. We need to do something before I really lose my temper!'

The clergyman agreed to speak with the boys, but asked to see them individually. The eight-year-old went to meet with him first. The clergyman sat the boy down and asked him sternly, 'Where is God?'

The boy made no response, so the clergyman repeated the question in an even sterner tone, 'Where is God?'

Again the boy made no attempt to answer. So the clergyman raised his voice even more and shook his finger in the boy's face, 'WHERE IS GOD?'

At that the boy bolted from the room and ran directly home to his bedroom.

His older brother followed him into the room and said, 'What happened?'

The younger brother replied, 'We are in *big* trouble this time! God is missing and they think we did it.'

> # The most important thing a father can do for his children is to love their mother.
>
> *Theodore Hesburgh*

Partnership

A man who says marriage is a 50–50 proposition doesn't understand two things: (1) women; and (2) fractions.

Patience

A man and a woman are on their honeymoon after a long and very happy courtship. On their honeymoon, they decide to take their horses through the beautiful mountain passes of Europe. As the horses are crossing a small stream, the woman's horse missteps and jostles her. Once across the stream, the man dismounts, walks over to the horse, and stares into its eyes. Finally, he states, 'That's one.' The man remounts his horse and they continue their ride.

A bit further down the path, the woman's horse stumbles when stepping over a fallen tree. The man dismounts, stares the horse in the eyes, and boldly states, 'That's two!' He returns to his saddle and they move on.

As the afternoon sun begins to set, the woman's horse once again loses its footing on a mossy slope. The man dismounts, moves to the woman's horse, and helps his wife out of the saddle. Moving to the front of the horse, he stares it in the eyes and firmly says, 'That's three.' Then he removes a pistol from his jacket and shoots the horse dead.

The woman, quite upset at seeing the beautiful horse killed, says to her husband, 'That's terrible! Why would you do such a thing?'

The man stares at his wife and firmly says, 'That's one!'

Perfection

There was a perfect man who met a perfect woman. After a perfect courtship, they had a perfect wedding. Their life together was, of course, perfect.

One snowy, stormy Christmas Eve, this perfect couple were driving their perfect car along a winding road, when they noticed someone at the roadside in distress. Being the perfect couple, they stopped to help.

There stood Santa Claus with a huge bundle of toys. Not wanting to disappoint any children on the eve of Christmas, the perfect couple loaded Santa and his toys into their vehicle. Soon they were driving along delivering the toys.

Unfortunately, the driving conditions deteriorated and the perfect couple and Santa Claus had an accident. Only one of them survived the accident. Who was the survivor?

The perfect woman. She's the only one who really existed in the first place. Everyone knows there is no Santa Claus and there is no such thing as a perfect man...

Permanence

Being in a long marriage is a little bit like that nice cup of coffee every morning – I might have it *every* day, but I still enjoy it.

Stephen Gaines

If you live to be a hundred, I want to live to be a hundred minus one day, so I never have to live without you.

Winnie the Pooh

The divorce rate would be lower if instead of marrying for better or worse people would marry for good.

Ruby Dee

Love seems the swiftest, but it is the slowest of all growths. No man or woman really knows what perfect love is until they have been married a quarter of a century.

Mark Twain

I think a man and a woman should choose each other for life, for the simple reason that a long life with all its accidents is barely enough time for a man and a woman to understand each other and... to understand – is to love.

William Butler Yeats

Get married.
Stay married.
What a concept!

The Snipe

One advantage of marriage, it seems to me, is that when you fall out of love with each other, it keeps you together until maybe you fall in love again.

Judith Viorst

New love is the brightest, and long love is the greatest, but revived love is the tenderest thing known on earth.

Thomas Hardy

A successful marriage requires falling in love many times, always with the same person.

Mignon McLaughlin

I knew couples who'd been married almost forever – forty, fifty, sixty years. Seventy-two, in one case. They'd be tending each other's illnesses, filling in each other's faulty memories, dealing with the money troubles or the daughter's suicide, or the grandson's drug addiction. And I was beginning to suspect that it made no difference whether they'd married the right person. Finally, you're just with who you're with. You've signed on with her, put in a half century with her, grown to know her as well as you know yourself or even better, and she's become the right person. Or the only person, might be more to the point. I wish someone had told me that earlier. I'd have hung on then; I swear I would.

Anne Tyler

What greater thing is there for two human souls than to feel that they are joined for life – to strengthen each other in all labour, to rest on each other in all sorrow, to minister to each other in all pain, to be one with each other in silent, unspeakable memories at the moment of the last parting.

George Eliot

Perseverance

I now think of marriage like I think about living in my home state of Minnesota. You move into marriage in the springtime of hope, but eventually arrive at the Minnesota winter, with its cold and darkness. Many of us are tempted to give up and move south at this point, not realizing that maybe we've hit a rough spot in a marriage that's actually above average. The problem with giving up, of course, is that our next marriage will enter its own winter at some point. So do we just keep moving on, or do we make our stand now – with this person, in this season? That's the moral, existential question we face when our marriage is in trouble.

Bill Doherty

Pillows

> *What a happy and holy fashion it is that those who love one another should rest on the same pillow.*
>
> Nathaniel Hawthorne

Potential

The challenge is to help couples turn 'I Do' into 'We Can'.

Scott Stanley

Practicalities

> *Marriage is not just spiritual communion; it is also remembering to take out the trash.*
>
> *Joyce Brothers*

Prayer

A near-sighted minister glanced at the note that Mrs Jones had sent to him by an usher.

The note read: 'Bill Jones having gone to sea, his wife desires the prayers of the congregation for his safety.'

Failing to observe the punctuation, he startled his audience by announcing: 'Bill Jones, having gone to see his wife, desires the prayers of the congregation for his safety.'

A wedding prayer

Lord Jesus, grant that I and my spouse may have a true and understanding love for each other. Grant that we may both be filled with faith and trust. Give us the grace to live with each other in peace and harmony.

May we always bear with one another's weaknesses and grow from each other's strengths. Help us to forgive one another's failings and grant us patience, kindness, cheerfulness and the spirit of placing the well-being of one another ahead of self.

May the love that brought us together grow and mature with each passing year. Bring us both ever closer to You through our love for each other. Let our love grow to perfection. Amen.

Some pray to marry the man they love,
My prayer will somewhat vary;
I humbly pray to Heaven above
That I love the man I marry.

Rose Stokes

A prayer for a married couple

O God, our Heavenly Father, protect and bless us. Deepen and strengthen our love for each other day by day. Grant that by Thy mercy neither of us ever say one unkind word to the other.

Forgive and correct our faults, and make us constantly to forgive one another should one of us unconsciously hurt the other. Make us and keep us sound and well in body, alert in mind, tender in heart, devout in spirit.

O Lord, grant us each to rise to the other's best. Then we pray Thee add to our common life such virtues as only Thou canst give.

And so, O Father, consecrate our life and our love completely to Thy worship, and to the service of all about us, especially those whom Thou has appointed us to serve, that we may always stand before Thee in happiness and peace; through Jesus Christ our Lord. Amen.

Bishop Slattery

Preparation

We took our time [preparing for marriage], we looked forward to it; didn't want to run into something and have nothing to count on but love...

Aunt May in Spiderman 3

Problems

> HUBBY: 'You always carry my photo in your handbag to the office. Why?'
>
> WIFE: 'When there is a problem, no matter how impossible, I look at your picture and the problem disappears.'
>
> HUBBY: 'You see how miraculous and powerful I am for you!'
>
> WIFE: 'Yes, I see your picture and say to myself, "What other problem can there be greater than this one?"'

Promises

I didn't marry you because you were perfect. I didn't even marry you because I loved you. I married you because you gave me a promise. That promise made up for your faults. And the promise I gave you made up for mine. Two imperfect people got married and it was the promise that made the marriage. And when our children were growing up, it wasn't a house that protected them; and it wasn't our love that protected them – it was that promise.

Thornton Wilder

Proposals

During his courtship with a young woman named Julia Dent, Ulysses S. Grant once took her out for a buggy ride. Coming to a flooded creek spanned by a flimsy bridge, Grant assured Julia that it was safe to cross. 'Don't be frightened,' he said. 'I'll look after you.'

'Well,' replied Julia, 'I shall cling to you whatever happens.'

True to her word, she clung tightly to Grant's arm as they drove safely across.

Grant drove on in thoughtful silence for a few minutes, then cleared his throat and said, 'Julia, you said back there that you would cling to me whatever happened. Would you like to cling to me for the rest of our lives?'

She would, and they were married in August 1848.

Put-downs

Do you and your spouse feed each other a steady diet of put-downs? If you do, your marriage could be headed for divorce court.

When psychologists Cliff Nortarius and Howard Markman studied newlyweds over the first decade of marriage, they discovered that couples who stayed together uttered 5 or fewer put-downs in every 100 comments to each other. But couples who inflicted twice as many verbal wounds – 10 or more putdowns out of every 100 comments – later split up.

Watch what you say! Little, nit-picking comments are like a cancer in marriage, slowly draining the life out of a committed relationship.

Dr James Dobson's Focus on the Family Bulletin

Quarrelling

'You're in incredible shape,' the doctor said. 'How old are you again?'

'I'm seventy-eight,' the man said.

'Seventy-eight?' asked the doctor. 'How do you stay so healthy? You look like a sixty-year-old.'

'Well,' the man explained, 'my wife and I made a pact when we got married that whenever she got mad with me, she would go into the kitchen and cool off and I would go outside to settle down.'

'What does that have to do with it?' asked the doctor.

'I've pretty much lived an outdoor life.'

"Of course, another plus is that we're practically self-sufficient."

HUSBAND: When I get mad at you, you never fight back. How do you control your anger?

WIFE: I clean the toilet bowl.

HUSBAND: How does that help?

WIFE: I use your toothbrush!

As a new bride, Aunt Edna moved into the small home on her husband's ranch. She put a shoebox on a shelf in her closet and asked her husband *never* to touch it.

For fifty years Uncle Jack left the box alone until Aunt Edna was old and dying. One day when he was putting their affairs in order, he found the box again and thought it might hold something important. Opening it, he found two doilies and £82,500 in cash.

He took the box to her and asked about the contents.

'My mother gave me that box the day we married,' she explained. 'She told me to make a doily to help ease my frustrations every time I got mad at you.'

Uncle Jack was very touched that in fifty years she'd only been mad at him twice.

'What's the £82,500 for?' he asked.

'Oh, that's the money I made selling the rest of the doilies.'

It is sometimes essential for a husband and a wife to quarrel — they get to know each other better.

Goethe

To keep your marriage brimming,
with love in the wedding cup,
whenever you're wrong, admit it;
whenever you're right, shut up.

Ogden Nash

A man complained to his friend, 'I just can't take it any more.'
His friend said, 'Well, what's wrong?'
The man replied, 'It's my wife. Every time we have an
argument, she gets historical.'
'You mean *hysterical*, don't you?'
'No, I mean *historical*. Every argument we have, she
always brings up the past.'

Never go to
bed mad.
Stay up and
fight.

Phyllis Diller

Three weeks after her wedding day, Joanna called her minister. 'Reverend,' she wailed, 'John and I had a *dreadful* fight!'

'Calm down, my child,' said the minister, 'it's not half as bad as you think it is. Every marriage has to have its first fight!'

'I know, I know!' said Joanna, 'but what am I going to do with the *body*?'

We were visiting friends when they received a telephone call from their recently married daughter. After several tense minutes on the phone, the mother told the father to pick up the extension. The newlyweds had had their first big fight.

In a few moments, the father rejoined us and tersely explained, 'Said she wanted to come home.'

'What did you tell her?' I asked.

'Told her she was home.'

Larry Cunningham

Rabbis

A man goes to see the Rabbi. 'Rabbi, something terrible is happening and I have to talk to you about it.'

The Rabbi asks, 'What's wrong?'

'My wife is poisoning me.'

The Rabbi, very surprised by this, asks, 'Are you sure? Why would she do such a thing?'

The man then pleads, 'I don't know why, but I'm telling you, I'm certain she's poisoning me. What should I do?'

The Rabbi thinks a bit, then says, 'Tell you what – let me talk to her. I'll see what I can find out and I'll let you know.'

A week later the Rabbi calls the man and says, 'Well, I spoke with your wife. I called her and we talked on the phone for three hours. You want my advice?'

'Yes, yes, of course,' says the man.

The Rabbi replies, 'Take the poison.'

Rings

At a cocktail party, one woman said to another, 'Aren't you wearing your wedding ring on the wrong finger?'

The other replied, 'Yes, I am. I married the wrong man.'

A businessman boarded a plane to find, sitting next to him, an elegant woman wearing the largest, most stunning diamond ring he had ever seen. He asked her about it.

'This is the Klopman diamond,' she said. 'It is beautiful, but there is a terrible curse that goes with it.'

'What's the curse?' the man asked.

'Mr Klopman.'

The minister receives the ring(s), and says this prayer...
Heavenly Father, by your blessing let *these rings* be to N and N a symbol of unending love and faithfulness, to remind them of the vow and covenant which they have made this day through Jesus Christ our Lord. **Amen.**

The bridegroom/bride places the ring on the fourth finger of the bride's/ bridegroom's left hand and, holding it there, says:
N, I give you this ring as a sign of our marriage. With my body I honour you, all that I am I give to you, and all that I have I share with you, within the love of God, Father, Son and Holy Spirit.

From the Wedding Service in Common Worship

A little boy was at a relative's wedding. As he was coming down the aisle he would take two steps, stop, and turn to the crowd (alternating between the bride's side and the groom's side). While facing the crowd, he would put his hands up like claws and roar loudly.

So it went – step, step, roar, step, step, roar – all the way down the aisle.

As you can imagine, the crowd was near tears from laughing so hard by the time he reached the front. The little boy, however, was getting more and more distressed by all the laughing, and was near tears himself by the time he reached the pulpit.

When asked what he was doing, the child sniffed and said, 'I was being the Ring Bear.'

Divorced couples in Albuquerque, New Mexico, can take advantage of a new business in town. The company is called Freedom Rings: Jewellery for the Divorced. Founded by jeweller and divorcee Lynn Peters, the company makes custom jewellery out of wedding rings. Each customer at Freedom Rings pays a fee, and the ring-smashing ceremony begins – complete with champagne and music. Just before the smashing the M.C. says, 'We will now release any remaining ties to your past by transforming your ring –which represents the past – into a token of your new beginning. Now take the hammer. Stop for a moment to consider the transformation that is about to begin your new life. Ready? With this swing let freedom ring!'

She then uses a four-pound sledgehammer to whack her emblem of love and fidelity into a shapeless piece of metal. And the ceremony ends.

Brian Peterson

An Irishman by the name of O'Mally proposed to his girl on St Patrick's Day. He gave her a ring with a synthetic diamond.

The excited young lass showed it to her father, a jeweller. He took one look at it and saw it wasn't real. The young lass, on learning it wasn't real, returned to her future husband. She protested vehemently about his cheapness.

'It was in honour of St Patrick's Day,' he smiled. 'I gave you a sham rock.'

Romance

Writers say that love is concerned only with young people, and the excitement and glamour of romance end at the altar. How blind they are. The best romance is inside marriage; the finest love stories come after the wedding, not before.

Irving Stone

Some people claim that marriage interferes with romance. There's no doubt about it. Any time you have a romance, your wife is bound to interfere.

Groucho Marx

Rules

Twelve rules for a happy marriage

1. Never both be angry at once.
2. Never yell at each other unless the house is on fire.
3. Remember that it takes two to make an argument. The one who is wrong is the one who will be doing most of the talking.
4. Yield to the wishes of the other – as an exercise in self-discipline, if you can't think of a better reason.
5. If you have a choice between making yourself or your mate look good –choose your mate.
6. If you feel you must criticize, do so lovingly.
7. Never bring up a mistake of the past.
8. Neglect the whole world rather than each other.
9. Never let the day end without saying at least one complimentary thing to your life partner.
10. Never meet without an affectionate greeting.
11. When you've made a mistake, talk it out and ask for forgiveness.
12. Never go to bed mad.

Ann Landers

Sacrifice

Dear friends, let us love one another, for love comes from God. Everyone who loves has been born of God and knows God. Whoever does not love does not know God, because God is love. This is how God showed his love among us: He sent his one and only Son into the world that we might live through him. This is love: not that we loved God, but that he loved us and sent his Son as an atoning sacrifice for our sins. Dear friends, since God so loved us, we also ought to love one another. No one has ever seen God; but if we love one another, God lives in us and his love is made complete in us.

We know that we live in him and he in us, because he has given us of his Spirit. And we have seen and testify that the Father has sent his Son to be the Saviour of the world. If anyone acknowledges that Jesus is the Son of God, God lives in him and he in God. And so we know and rely on the love God has for us.

God is love. Whoever lives in love lives in God, and God in him. In this way, love is made complete among us so that we will have confidence on the day of judgment, because in this world we are like him. There is no fear in love. But perfect love drives out fear, because fear has to do with punishment. The one who fears is not made perfect in love.

1 John 4:7–18, NIV

Sanity

Marriage is a great institution, but I'm not ready for an institution.

Mae West

A psychiatrist visited a California mental institution and asked a patient, 'How did you get here? What was the nature of your illness?'

He got the following reply: 'Well, it all started when I got married, and I guess I should never have done it. I married a widow with a grown daughter who then became my stepdaughter. My dad came to visit us, fell in love with my lovely stepdaughter, then married her. And so my stepdaughter was now my stepmother. Soon, my wife had a son who was, of course, my daddy's brother-in-law since he is the half-brother of my stepdaughter, who is now, of course, my daddy's wife.

'So, as I told you, when my stepdaughter married my daddy, she was at once my stepmother! Now, since my new son is brother to my stepmother, he also became my uncle. As you know, my wife is my step-grandmother since she is my stepmother's mother. Don't forget that my stepmother is my stepdaughter. Remember, too, that I am my wife's grandson.

'But hold on just a few minutes more. You see, since I'm married to my step-grandmother, I am not only my wife's grandson and her hubby, but I am also my own grandfather. Now can you understand how I got put in this place?'

After staring blankly with a dizzy look on his face, the psychiatrist replied: 'Move over!'

Service

In the musical *Fiddler on the Roof*, Tevye, a man devoted to tradition, finds his thinking challenged when his oldest daughter wants to marry for love, instead of having her marriage arranged by her parents.

It had never occurred to him that one would marry for love, and one night he cannot help but ask his own wife the question (in song, of course!): 'Do You Love Me?'

TEVYE: 'Golde, do you love me?'
GOLDE: 'Do I what?'
Tevye: 'Do you love me?'
GOLDE: 'You're a fool!'
TEVYE: 'I know! But do you love me?'
GOLDE: 'Do I love him? For twenty-five years I've cooked for him, cleaned for him, starved with him. Twenty-five years my bed is his. If that's not love – what is?'

Snobbery

A married couple trying to live up to a snobbish lifestyle went to a party. The conversation turned to Mozart: 'Absolutely brilliant, magnificent, a genius!'

The woman, wanting to join in the conversation, remarked casually, 'Ah, Mozart. You're so right. I love him. Only this morning I saw him getting on the No. 5 bus going to Chelsea.'

There was a sudden hush, and everyone looked at her. Her husband was mortified. He pulled her away and whispered, 'We're leaving right now. Get your coat and let's get out of here.'

As they drove home, he kept muttering to himself. Finally his wife turned to him. 'You're angry about something.'

'Oh really? You noticed?' he sneered. 'I've never been so embarrassed in my life! You saw Mozart take the No. 5 bus to Chelsea? You idiot! Don't you know the No. 5 bus doesn't go to Chelsea?'

Stages

Reflections on 'The Couple's Journey'

The romance stage. Two people's individual fantasies come together and fertilize each other. A shared dream is conceived.

The power struggle stage springs from the seeds of disappointment sown by the hands of wishful thinking and selective perceiving. For the struggle to flourish, it requires a soil rich in unacknowledged demands and accumulated resentments.

The stability stage provides insights into understanding our struggles. We recognize the mirror in each other, stop blaming the other and start focusing on the power struggles within. We discover, as long as conflicts are unresolved within me, they will be expressed as conflicts between us. Stability represents not sameness or continual peace so much as an attitude of acceptance: acceptance of the other as a real, live separate other, who may not always meet my expectations; and acceptance of the parts of myself that create such expectations.

Commitment means taking responsibility for making it work. We let go of 'if onlys' and start to make conscious choices of how we respond. We both support each other's self-expression in the knowledge that 'my truth serves your truth' (John Welwood). We learn to live with our differences, our mistakes and become discerning about when to do what in the service of our aim.

The co-creation stage involves two central developments: The ability to choicefully respond to the environment in a way that recognizes our impact on it and its impact on us. The ability to relate to the world outside with the same sense of mutual responsibility and responsiveness that we share with our partner.

Mirjam Busch

Stages in a relationship

A Man, a Woman, and a Cat. At the beginning of a relationship...

WOMAN: Darling, I'd like you to meet my cat.
MAN: (*Under his breath:* Ugh. I hate cats.) Uh, hi. Nice kitty.

As the relationship progresses...

WOMAN: Dear, I get the impression that you don't like my cat.
MAN: That's ridiculous. I love Poopsie. (*Under his breath:* This cat is ruining our relationship.)

As the relationship reaches a more stable level...

WOMAN: Oh, Poopsie looks just so cute sitting there on your lap.
MAN: (Darn thing's shedding all over my new suit.) Well, I guess she's not so bad.

Later...

WOMAN: I swear, you like that cat more than you like me.
MAN: You know that's not true. I can't help it if she follows me around all the time.

The final stage...

MAN: Honey, have you seen my cat anywhere?
WOMAN: What do you mean, *your* cat?

Success

The seven secrets of a successful marriage

Secret 1: Successful married couples get their deal straight. Successful couples talk deeply before the wedding about their expectations of each other, and if there's serious disagreement – for example, he wants kids, she doesn't – they think seriously about whether to marry.

Secret 2: Successful married couples keep their individuality. Successful couples know that, however much love there is, marriage can bring this trapped feeling. They encourage each other not to be always 'us', to take 'me' time, to have 'me' hobbies and even 'me' friends.

Secret 3: Successful married couples keep each other centre stage. Successful couples always keep each other centre stage. They are interested in their partner's opinions. They take their partner seriously. They refer to their spouse in glowing terms when talking to other people.

Secret 4: Successful married couples learn to resolve conflicts. Successful couples keep communicating, whatever the bad feeling between them. They negotiate differences and disagreements so that they both end up getting a fair deal.

Secret 5: Successful married couples keep the passion alive. Successful couples stay affectionate. If there's a sexual drought, they ride it out by flirting, touching, hugging, kissing and being romantic.

Secret 6: Successful married couples grow with each other. Successful couples anticipate shifts and ride with them. Rather than demanding they both stay the same forever, they welcome the natural developments of personality and partnership that happen with time.

Secret 7: Successful married couples keep working at it. Successful couples take rain checks and keep having regular 'where are we at' conversations to make sure that they're both happy with the way things are going.

Susan Quilliam

Threads

Chains do not hold a marriage together. It is threads, hundreds of tiny threads, which sew people together through the years.

Simone Signoret

Time

The greatest weakness of most humans is their hesitancy to tell others how much they love them while they're still alive.

Olando Battista

Love is a four-letter word spelled T-I-M-E.

Anon

If we discovered that we had five minutes left to say all we wanted to say, every telephone booth would be occupied by people calling other people to stammer that they love them. Why wait until the last five minutes?

C. Morley

You can run several agendas in life, but you cannot run them all at a hundred per cent without someone paying the price. We have so many excuses. The main one is that we convince ourselves that a slower day is coming. We say to ourselves, 'When the house is decorated, when I get my promotion, when I pass those exams – then I'll have more time.' Every time we have to say, 'Not now, darling...' we tell ourselves it's okay because that slower day is getting nearer. It's as well that we realize, here and now, that the slower day is an illusion – it never comes. Whatever our situation, we all have the potential to fill up our time. That's why we need to make time for the things that we believe are important – and we need to make it now.

Rob Parsons

Toasts

A toast from the father of the bride

I wish for you (and for me) many beautiful babies.

I wish for you ever stronger collaborations, teamwork and partnerships.

I wish for you long conversations – and short fights – which inexorably and successfully move the whole mass forward.

I wish for you that you always laugh at each other's jokes and understand each other's prose.

I wish for you good health in each other's arms.

I wish for you fidelity – especially in trying times. It's the crucial link that holds it all together.

I wish for you romantic marriage vacations – time away for just the two of you. During which I promise to babysit all those beautiful babies.

And I wish for you, finally, the full joy of reaching the end together – that bittersweet moment when in death you shall part.

Togetherness

Let there be spaces in your togetherness.

Kahlil Gibran

A long marriage is two people trying to dance a duet and two solos at the same time.

Anne Taylor Fleming

Don't smother each other.
No one can grow in shade.

Leo Buscaglia

Transformation

An Amish boy and his father were visiting a mall. They were amazed by almost everything they saw, but especially by two shiny, silver walls that could move apart and back together again.

The boy asked, 'What is this, Father?'

The father (never having seen an elevator) responded, 'Son, I have never seen anything like this in my life. I don't know what it is.'

While the boy and his father were watching with amazement, an old lady in a wheelchair rolled up to the moving walls and pressed a button. The walls opened and the lady rolled between them into a small room. The walls closed and the boy and his father watched the small circular numbers above the walls light up sequentially. They continued to watch until it reached the last number, and then these numbers began to light in reverse order. The walls opened up again and a beautiful young woman stepped out.

The father, not taking his eyes off the young woman, said quietly to his son, 'Quick! Go get your Mother.'

Any fool can have a trophy wife.
It takes a real man to have
a trophy marriage.

Diane Sollee

The development of a really good marriage is
not a natural process. It is an achievement.

David and Vera Mace

Unselfishness

What do we live
for, if it is not to
make life less
difficult for each
other?

George Eliot

Many years ago, the Salvation Army was holding an international convention, and their founder, General William Booth, could not attend because of physical weakness. He cabled his convention message to them. It was one word: 'OTHERS'.

What else is love but understanding and rejoicing in the fact that another person lives, acts, and experiences otherwise than we do?

Friedrich Nietzsche

Dearest Jimmy,

No words could ever express the great unhappiness I've felt since breaking our engagement. Please say you'll take me back. No one could ever take your place in my heart, so please forgive me. I love you, I love you, I love you!

Yours forever, Marie

P.S.: And congratulations on winning the lottery.

"Been a bit of a Jack-the-lad, have we sir? Special Delivery, sign here."

In 1921 Lewis Lawes became the warden at Sing Sing Prison. No prison was tougher than Sing Sing during that time. But when Warden Lawes retired some 20 years later, that prison had become a humanitarian institution. Those who studied the system said credit for the change belonged to Lawes. But when he was asked about the transformation, here's what he said: 'I owe it all to my wonderful wife, Catherine, who is buried outside the prison walls.'

Catherine Lawes was a young mother with three small children when her husband became the warden. Everybody warned her from the beginning that she should never set foot inside the prison walls, but that didn't stop Catherine! When the first prison basketball game was held, she went... walking into the gym with her three beautiful kids and she sat in the stands with the inmates.

Her attitude was: 'My husband and I are going to take care of these men and I believe they will take care of me! I don't have to worry.'

She insisted on getting acquainted with them and their records. She discovered one convicted murderer was blind so she paid him a visit. Holding his hand in hers she said, 'Do you read Braille?' 'What's Braille?' he asked. Then she taught him how to read. Years later he would weep in love for her.

Later, Catherine found a deaf-mute in prison. She went to school to learn how to use sign language. Many said that Catherine Lawes was the presence of Jesus that came alive again in Sing Sing from 1921 to 1937.

Then, she was killed in a car accident. The next morning Lewis Lawes didn't come to work, so the acting warden took his place. It seemed almost instantly that the prison knew something was wrong.

The following day, her body was resting in a casket in her home, three-quarters of a mile from the prison. As the acting warden took his early morning walk he was shocked to see a large crowd of the toughest, hardest-looking criminals gathered like a herd of animals at the main gate. He came closer and noted tears of grief and sadness. He knew how much they loved Catherine. He turned and faced the men, 'All right, men, you can go. Just be sure and check in tonight!' Then he opened the gate and a parade of criminals walked, without a guard, the three-quarters of a mile to stand in line to pay their final respects to Catherine Lawes. And every one of them checked back in. Every one!

Tim Kimmel

A bell is no bell 'til you ring it,
A song is no song 'til you sing it,
And love in your heart
Wasn't put there to stay —
Love isn't love
'Til you give it away.

The Sound of Music

Valentines

After she woke up, a woman told her husband, 'I just dreamed that you gave me a pearl necklace for Valentine's Day. What do you think it means?'

'You'll know tonight,' he said.

That evening, the man came home with a small package and gave it to his wife. Delighted, she opened it – to find a book entitled *The Meaning of Dreams*.

An old man got on a bus one February the 14th, carrying a dozen roses. He sat beside a young man. The young man looked at the roses and said, 'Somebody's going to get a beautiful Valentine's Day gift.'

'Yes,' said the old man.

A few minutes went by and the old man noticed that his young companion was staring at the roses. 'Do you have a girlfriend?' the old man asked.

'I do,' said the young man. 'I'm going to see her right now, and I'm going to give her this Valentine's Day card.'

They rode in silence for another ten minutes, and then the old man got up to get off the bus. As he stepped out into the aisle, he suddenly placed the roses on the young man's lap and said, 'I think my wife would want you to have these. I'll tell her that I gave them to you.'

He left the bus quickly. As the bus pulled away, the young man turned to see the old man enter the gates of a cemetery.

These are entries to a competition asking for a rhyme with the most romantic first line but the least romantic second line:

I thought that I could love no other –
Until, that is, I met your brother.

Roses are red, violets are blue, sugar is sweet, and so are you.
But the roses are wilting, the violets are dead,
the sugar bowl's empty and so is your head.

Of loving beauty you float with grace;
If only you could hide your face.

Kind, intelligent, loving and hot –
This describes everything you are not.

I want to feel your sweet embrace,
But don't take that paper bag off of your face.

I love your smile, your face, and your eyes –
Damn, I'm good at telling lies!

My darling, my lover, my beautiful wife:
Marrying you screwed up my life.

I see your face when I am dreaming;
That's why I always wake up screaming.

What inspired this amorous rhyme?
Two parts vodka, one part lime.

Virtues

Therefore, as God's chosen people, holy and dearly loved, clothe yourselves with compassion, kindness, humility, gentleness and patience. Bear with each other and forgive whatever grievances you may have against one another. Forgive as the Lord forgave you. And over all these virtues put on love, which binds them all together in perfect unity.

Colossians 3:12–14, NIV

Vision

At the opening of Disney World, Florida, Mrs Walt Disney gave the inaugural speech, her husband being dead. An interviewer said to her, 'I wish Dr Disney had lived to see it.'

Mrs Disney replied, 'He did.'

Life has taught us that love does not consist in gazing at each other but in looking outward together in the same direction.

Antoine De Saint-Exupery

The goal in marriage is not to think alike, but to think together.

Robert Dodds

Vows

The minister says to the couple: The vows you are about to take are to be made in the presence of God, who is judge of all and knows all the secrets of our hearts; therefore if either of you knows a reason why you may not lawfully marry, you must declare it now.

The minister says to the bridegroom: N, will you take N to be your wife? Will you love her, comfort her, honour and protect her, and, forsaking all others, be faithful to her as long as you both shall live?

He answers: I will.

The minister says to the bride: N, will you take N to be your husband? Will you love him, comfort him, honour and protect him, and, forsaking all others, be faithful to him as long as you both shall live?

She answers: I will.

The minister says to the congregation: Will you, the families and friends of N and N, support and uphold them in their marriage now and in the years to come?

We will.

The bride and bridegroom face each other. The bridegroom takes the bride's right hand in his. These words... are used:
I, N, take you, N, to be my wife, to have and to hold from this day forward; for better, for worse, for richer, for poorer, in sickness and in health, to love and to cherish, till death us do part; according to God's holy law. In the presence of God I make this vow.

They loose hands. The bride takes the bridegroom's right hand in hers, and says:
I, N, take you, N, to be my husband, to have and to hold from this day forward; for better, for worse, for richer, for poorer, in sickness and in health, to love and to cherish, till death us do part; according to God's holy law. In the presence of God I make this vow.

From the Wedding Service in
Common Worship

A grandmother overheard her five-year-old granddaughter playing 'wedding'. The wedding vows went like this:

'You have the right to remain silent. Anything you say may be held against you. You have the right to have an attorney present. You may kiss the bride.'

*D*uring the wedding rehearsal, the groom approached the minister with an unusual offer:

'Look, I'll give you £100 if you'll change the wedding vows. When you get to the part where I'm supposed to promise to "love, honour and worship" and "be faithful to her forever", I'd appreciate it if you'd just leave that out.'

He passed the minister £100 and walked away satisfied. On the day of the wedding, when it came time for the groom's vows, the minister looked the young man in the eye and said:

'Will you promise to prostrate yourself before her, obey her every command and wish, serve her breakfast in bed every morning of your life, and swear eternally before God and your lovely wife that you will not ever even look at another woman, as long as you both shall live?'

The groom gulped and looked around, and said in a tiny voice, 'Yes,' then leaned toward the minister and hissed: 'I thought we had a deal.'

The minister put a £100 into the groom's hand and whispered: 'She made me a better offer.'

Waiting

Women spend two years and nine months of their lives getting ready to go out. Meanwhile, men spend three months of their lives waiting for their wives to get ready!

Weddings

All weddings are similar, but every marriage is different.

John Berger

A little boy was attending his first wedding. After the service, his younger cousin asked him, 'How many women can a man marry?'

'Sixteen,' the boy responded.

His cousin was amazed that he had answered so quickly. 'How do you know that?'

'Easy,' the little boy said. 'All you have to do is add it up, like the preacher said: "Four better, four worse, four richer, four poorer."'

"I <u>heard</u> that Derek. 'Chance'd be a fine thing!' "

A little girl at a wedding asked, 'Mummy, why do brides always wear white?'

The mother replied, 'Because they're happy, dear.'

Halfway through the wedding the girl whispered, 'Mummy, if brides wear white because they're happy, then why do men wear black?'

A man went to a friend's wedding and was very impressed with the choice of hymns, especially 'Love Divine'. He was due to be married himself a few months later, so he made a note of the number: 343.

When he next met with the minister who was to conduct his wedding, he told him he would like hymn 343.

'Are you sure?' asked the minister. 'It's rather an unusual choice!'

'No, I'm certain. I heard it at my friend's wedding, and it is just what I want to say', insisted the man.

What he had not realized was that his friend was married in a Methodist church, using the Methodist hymn book, whereas at his wedding they were using *Hymns Ancient and Modern*.

Imagine the surprise of all – not least the bride – when they started to sing *Hymns Ancient and Modern* 343:

> Come, O thou traveller unknown
> whom still I hold, but cannot see;
> my company before is gone
> and I am left alone with thee;
> With thee all night I mean to stay,
> and wrestle till the break of day.

From a US News Report

Undercover police, staging the wedding of 'a drug kingpin's daughter', let it be known on the street that dealers were 'invited' (i.e. expected) to attend.

The bride and groom were police, as were the band, the bartender, and about half the guests. The band playing at the wedding was 'S.P.O.C.' (C.O.P.S. backwards), and the wedding went through the full ceremony, including the dancing afterwards.

The long-sought dealers were arrested after the 'band' took their break. The last song the band played before taking their break? 'I Fought the Law, and the Law Won'.

Loving you is a wonderful way
to spend a lifetime!

Anon

Dance through
life with me – the
best is yet to be.

Anon

What's the earth with all its art, verse, music worth – compared with love, found, gained, and kept?

Robert Browning

What greater thing is there for two human souls than to feel that they are joined for life.

George Eliot

Two hearts once joined in friendship, united now with love.

Anon

When Adam was lonely, God created for him not ten friends, but one wife.

Anon

The joining of two hands makes one heart!

Anon

Let our love be like an arch – two weaknesses learning together to form one strength.

Anon

Love is a flower which turns into fruit at marriage.

Finnish proverb

Life is a journey, and I'm so glad we're travelling together!

Anon

Henceforth there shall be
such a oneness between you,
that when one weeps,
the other will taste salt.

Anon

*We may not have it all together,
but together we have it all.*

Anon

God is
a great
matchmaker.

Jewish proverb

God, the best maker of all marriages,
Combine your hearts into one.

William Shakespeare

During the weeks before a girl's wedding, she was terribly anxious about making some mistakes at the ceremony. The minister reassured her several times, pointing out that the service was not difficult and she would do just fine.

'All you have to remember,' he said, 'is that when you enter the church you walk up the *aisle*. The groom and best man will be waiting before the *altar*. Then I shall request the congregation to sing a *hymn*. Then we shall get on with the ceremony. All you have to remember is the order in which those things happen, and you can't go wrong.'

The happy day finally arrived, and the bridegroom waited nervously for his bride to appear.

When she arrived and stood alongside him, he heard her quietly repeating to herself, 'Aisle, altar, hymn, aisle, altar, hymn.'

Witness

Why is it that people get married? Because we need a witness to our lives. There's a billion people on the planet. What does any one life really mean? But in a marriage, you're promising to care about everything... The good things, the bad things, the terrible things, the mundane things, all of it... all the time, every day. You're saying, 'Your life will not go unnoticed because I will notice it. Your life will not go unwitnessed – because I will be your witness.'

From the movie Shall We Dance? *(2004)*

Wives

There's a charming story that Thomas Wheeler, CEO of the Massachusetts Mutual Life Insurance Company, tells about himself. He and his wife were driving along an interstate highway when he noticed that their car was low on petrol. Wheeler got off the highway at the next exit and soon found a run-down petrol station with just one pump. He asked the lone attendant to fill the tank and check the oil, then went for a little walk around the station to stretch his legs.

As he was returning to the car, he noticed that the attendant and his wife were engaged in an animated conversation. The conversation stopped as he paid the attendant. But as he was getting back into the car, he saw the attendant wave and heard him say, 'It was great talking to you.'

As they drove out of the station, Wheeler asked his wife if she knew the man. She readily admitted that she did. They had gone to high school together and had dated steadily for about a year.

'Boy, were you lucky that I came along,' bragged Wheeler. 'If you had married him, you'd be the wife of a petrol station attendant instead of the wife of a chief executive officer.'

'My dear,' replied his wife, 'if I had married him, he'd be the chief executive officer and you'd be the petrol station attendant.'

Bishop Taylor brilliantly captured the sentiment of Proverbs 31 when he wrote: 'If you are for pleasure, marry. If you prize rosy health, marry. A good wife is heaven's last best gift to a man; his angel of mercy; minister of graces innumerable; his gem of many virtues; his box of jewels; her voice, his sweetest music; her smiles, his brightest day; her kiss, the guardian of innocence; her arms, the pale of his safety; the balm of his health; the balsam of his life; her industry, his surest wealth; her economy, his safest steward; her lips, his faithful counsellors… and her prayers, the ablest advocates of heaven's blessing on his head.'

A wife of noble character who can find?
She is worth far more than rubies.
Her husband has full confidence in her
and lacks nothing of value.
She brings him good, not harm,
all the days of her life.
She selects wool and flax
and works with eager hands.
She is like the merchant ships,
bringing her food from afar.
She gets up while it is still dark;
she provides food for her family
and portions for her servant girls.
She considers a field and buys it;
out of her earnings she plants a vineyard.
She sets about her work vigorously;
her arms are strong for her tasks.
She sees that her trading is profitable,
and her lamp does not go out at night.
In her hand she holds the distaff
and grasps the spindle with her fingers.
She opens her arms to the poor
and extends her hands to the needy.
When it snows, she has no fear for her household;
for all of them are clothed in scarlet.
She makes coverings for her bed;
she is clothed in fine linen and purple.
Her husband is respected at the city gate,
where he takes his seat among the elders of the land.
She makes linen garments and sells them,
and supplies the merchants with sashes.
She is clothed with strength and dignity;
she can laugh at the days to come.
She speaks with wisdom,
and faithful instruction is on her tongue.
She watches over the affairs of her household
and does not eat the bread of idleness.
Her children arise and call her blessed;
her husband also, and he praises her:
'Many women do noble things,
but you surpass them all.'
Charm is deceptive, and beauty is fleeting;
but a woman who fears the Lord is to be praised.
Give her the reward she has earned,
and let her works bring her praise at the city gate.

Proverbs 31:10–31, NIV

Women

A man walking along a California beach was deep in prayer. All of a sudden, he said out loud, 'Lord, grant me one wish.'

The sky clouded above his head and in a booming voice, the Lord said, 'Because you have tried to be faithful to me in all ways, I will grant you one wish.'

The man said, 'Build a bridge to Hawaii so I can drive over anytime I want.'

The Lord said, 'Your request is very materialistic. Think of the enormous challenges for that kind of undertaking. The supports required to reach the bottom of the Pacific! The concrete and steel it would take! I can do it, but it is hard for me to justify your desire for worldly things. Take a little more time and think of another wish, a wish you think would honour and glorify me.'

The man thought about it for a long time.

Finally he said, 'Lord, I wish that I could understand women. I want to know how they feel inside, what they are thinking when they give the silent treatment, why they cry, what they mean when they say "nothing", and how I can make a woman truly happy.'

The Lord replied, 'You want two lanes or four lanes on that bridge?'

A man walked into a bookshop and asked the woman behind the counter, 'Have you got a book called, *Man, the Master of Women*?'

'Try the fiction section,' said the woman.

What women want in a man, original list (age 22)

(1) Handsome. (2) Charming. (3) Financially successful. (4) A caring listener. (5) Witty. (6) In good shape. (7) Dresses with style. (8) Appreciates finer things. (9) Full of thoughtful surprises. (10) An imaginative, romantic lover.

What women want in a man, revised list (age 32)

(1) Nice looking (would prefer hair on his head). (2) Opens car doors, holds chairs. (3) Has enough money for a nice dinner. (4) Listens more than he talks. (5) Laughs at my jokes. (6) Carries bags of groceries with ease. (7) Owns at least one tie. (8) Appreciates a good home-cooked meal. (9) Remembers birthdays and anniversaries. (10) Seeks romance at least once a week.

What women want in a man, revised list (age 42)

(1) Not too ugly (bald head OK). (2) Doesn't drive off until I'm in the car. (3) A steady worker – splurges on dinner out occasionally. (4) Nods his head when I'm talking. (5) Usually remembers the punchlines of jokes. (6) Is in good enough shape to rearrange the furniture. (7) Wears a shirt that covers his stomach. (8) Knows not to buy champagne in screw-top bottles.

(9) Remembers to put the toilet-seat down. (10) Shaves most weekends.

What women want in a man, revised list (age 52)

(1) Keeps hair in nose and ears trimmed. (2) Doesn't belch or scratch in public. (3) Doesn't borrow money too often. (4) Doesn't nod off to sleep when I'm venting. (5) Doesn't re-tell the same joke too many times. (6) Is in good enough shape to get off the couch at weekends. (7) Usually wears matching socks and fresh underwear. (8) Appreciates a good TV dinner. (9) Remembers my name on occasion. (10) Shaves some weekends.

What women want in a man, revised list (age 62)

(1) Doesn't scare small children. (2) Remembers where the bathroom is. (3) Doesn't require much money for upkeep. (4) Only snores lightly when asleep. (5) Remembers why he's laughing. (6) Is in good enough shape to stand up by himself. (7) Usually wears some clothes. (8) Likes soft foods. (9) Remembers where he left his teeth. (10) Remembers that it's the weekend.

What women want in a man, revised list (age 72)

(1) Breathing.

The beauty of a woman
Is not in the clothes she wears,
The figure that she carries,
Or the way she combs her hair.
The beauty of a woman
Must be seen in her eyes,
Because that is the doorway to her heart,
The place where love resides.

The beauty of a woman
Is not in a facial mole,
But true beauty in a woman
Is reflected in her soul.
It is the caring that she lovingly gives,
The passion that she shows,
And the beauty of a woman
With passing years only grows!

Wonder

For two people in a marriage to live together day after day is unquestionably the one miracle the Vatican has overlooked.

Bill Cosby, Love and Marriage

Words

Astronaut Michael Collins, speaking at a banquet, quoted the estimate that the average man speaks 25,000 words a day and the average woman 30,000. Then he added: 'Unfortunately, when I come home each day I've spoken my 25,000 – and my wife hasn't started her 30,000.'

A couple had been debating the purchase of a new car for weeks. He wanted a new truck. She wanted a fast little sports-like car so she could zip through traffic around town. He would probably have settled on any beaten-up old truck, but everything she seemed to like was way out of their price range.

'Look!' she said. 'I want something that goes from 0 to 100 in 4 seconds or less. And my birthday is coming up. You could surprise me.'

So, for her birthday, he bought her a brand-new bathroom scale.

Services will be at the local Funeral Home on Monday the 12th. Please send your donations to the 'Think Before You Say Things To Your Wife Foundation'.

The bonds of marriage aren't worth much unless the interest is kept up.

Anon

There is such pleasure in long-term marriage that I really would hate to be my age and not have had a long-term marriage. Remember, sustaining a pleasurable, long-term marriage takes effort, deliberateness and an intention to learn about one another. In other words, marriage is for grown-ups.

Cokie Roberts

Love is a feeling, Marriage is a contract, and a Relationship is work.

Lori Gordon

All those 'and they lived happily ever after' fairy-tale endings need to be changed to 'and they began the very hard work of making their marriages happy.'

Linda Miles

Coming together is the beginning. Keeping together is progress. Working together is success.

Henry Ford

X-Rated!

How beautiful you are, my darling!
Oh, how beautiful!
Your eyes behind your veil are doves.
Your hair is like a flock of goats
descending from Mount Gilead.
Your teeth are like a flock of sheep just shorn,
coming up from the washing.
Each has its twin;
not one of them is alone.
Your lips are like a scarlet ribbon;
your mouth is lovely.
Your temples behind your veil
are like the halves of a pomegranate.
Your neck is like the tower of David,
built with elegance;
on it hang a thousand shields,
all of them shields of warriors.
Your two breasts are like two fawns,
like twin fawns of a gazelle
that browse among the lilies.
Until the day breaks
and the shadows flee,
I will go to the mountain of myrrh
and to the hill of incense.
All beautiful you are, my darling;
there is no flaw in you.

Song of Songs 4:1–7, NIV

A newly wed couple had just arrived in their honeymoon suite. After unpacking, the husband took off his trousers.

'Put these on,' he said to his wife.

She did and they were obviously much too large. 'There's no way I can wear these – they're way too big,' she said.

'Good! Now you know who wears the trousers in this family,' replied the husband.

Flustered, the wife removed her knickers and, handing them to her husband, said, 'Put these on.'

The husband looked at the tiny knickers and said, 'There's no way I can get into these.'

To which the wife replied, 'You're right – at least, not until you change your attitude!'

Before marriage, a girl has to make love to a man to hold him. After marriage, she has to hold him to make love to him.

Marilyn Monroe

One of the most talked about films of 1999 was Stanley Kubrick's *Eyes Wide Shut*, starring Tom Cruise and Nicole Kidman. It was Stanley Kubrick's final film, and one in which he explores the nature of sexuality, desire and intimacy. It's also very explicit.

Tom Cruise plays a successful young doctor, Bill Harford and Kidman plays his wife, Alice. They've been married nine years, have a daughter, have money, and seemingly have it all.

Then one night at a party both engage in a bit of flirtation. When they get home Alice reveals that she once had a very powerful sexual fantasy about a man she saw in a hotel. She'd never met the man before, she never acted on the fantasy, but it seemed so powerful she had actually imagined herself leaving Bill to pursue it. Bill is shocked, and throughout the rest of the film we find him giving in to his own desires. He has an encounter with a prostitute, and as he spirals further and further into a web of depravity, he ends up at an invitation-only orgy that exposes him to the extremes of sexual desire and almost gets him killed.

Paralleling Bill's sexual journey is the declining intimacy in his marriage. The sexual tension and deceit push Bill and Alice further apart, until towards the end of the movie they both realize just how destructive this sexual web has been, how close they've come to surrendering all that is good in their relationship. The film closes with an act of forgiveness in which Alice tells Bill that she loves him and that they need to make love.

Critics debate exactly what Kubrick was trying to say in the movie, but I think that one of the messages is the power of sexual desire to be constructive and destructive in our relationships. We learn that dark sexual desire lurks in the most unsuspected places – in ourselves, in our partners, in the very everyday people around us. Kubrick wants us to see how powerful these are, how they can ensnare even the best of us. We discover that darker sexual desires can be exhilarating when fulfilled, but that they are ultimately empty when compared to the genuine emotional intimacy of a good marriage relationship. And I think the end of the movie makes clear the need to preserve our marriages from sexual depravity through a passionate pursuit of desire within the relationship.

Scott Higgins

The Vicar decided to do something a little different one Sunday morning. He said, 'Today, I am going to say a single word and you are going to help me preach. Whatever single word I say, I want you to sing whatever hymn comes to your mind.'

So he shouted out 'Cross!' Immediately, the congregation started singing in unison 'The Old Rugged Cross'.

He shouted out 'Grace!' The congregation began to sing 'Amazing Grace'.

He said 'Power!' The congregation sang 'There Is Power in the Blood'.

The Vicar finally said 'Sex!' The congregation fell into total silence. Everyone was in shock. They all nervously began to look around at each other, afraid to say anything.

Then all of a sudden, from the back of the church, a little 88-year-old grandmother stood up and began to sing 'Memories'.

A man doing market research knocked on a door and was greeted by a young woman with three small children running around at her feet. He said, 'I'm doing some research for Vaseline. Have you ever used the product?'

She said, 'Yes. My husband and I use it all the time.'

'And if you don't mind me asking, what do you use it for?'

'We use it for sex.'

The researcher was a little taken aback. He said, 'Usually people lie to me and say that they use it on a child's bicycle chain or to help with a gate hinge. But, in fact, I know that most people do use it for sex. I admire you for your honesty. Since you've been frank so far, can you tell me exactly how you use it for sex?'

The woman said, 'I don't mind telling you at all. My husband and I put it on the door-knob and it keeps the kids out.'

A newly married sailor was informed by the Navy that he was going to be stationed a long way from home on a remote island in the Pacific for a year. A few weeks after he got there he began to miss his new wife, so he wrote her a letter.

'My love,' he wrote, 'we are going to be apart for a very long time. Already I'm starting to miss you and there's really not much to do here in the evenings. Besides that, we're constantly surrounded by young attractive native girls. Do you think if I had a hobby of some kind I would not be tempted?'

So his wife sent him back a harmonica, saying, 'Why don't you learn to play this?'

Eventually his tour of duty came to an end and he rushed back to his wife. 'Darling,' he said, 'I can't wait to see you for a cuddle!'

She kissed him and said, 'First, let's see you play that harmonica.'

The minister was passing a group of teenagers sitting on the church lawn, and he stopped to ask what they were doing.

'Nothing much, Pastor,' replied one lad. 'We're just seeing who can tell the biggest lie about their sex life.'

'Boys!' he exclaimed. 'I'm shocked. When I was your age, I never even thought about sex at all.'

They all replied, pretty much in unison, 'You win, Pastor!'

When the Apollo Mission astronaut Neil Armstrong first walked on the moon, he not only gave his famous 'One small step for man, one giant leap for mankind' statement, but followed it by several remarks – mostly routine conversation with other astronauts.

Just before he re-entered the lunar lander, however, he made the enigmatic remark, 'Good luck, Mr Gorsky.'

Many people at NASA thought it was a casual remark concerning some rival Soviet cosmonaut. However, upon checking, there was no Gorsky in either the Russian or the American space programmes.

Over the years many people questioned Armstrong as to what the 'Good luck, Mr Gorsky' statement meant, but Armstrong always just smiled and dodged the question.

On 5 July 1995 in Tampa Bay, Florida, while answering questions following a speech, a reporter asked Armstrong the twenty-six-year-old question. This time he finally responded. Mr Gorsky had died, and so Armstrong felt he could answer the question.

When he was a child, he was playing baseball with a friend in his back garden. His friend hit a fly ball, which landed in front of the neighbours' bedroom window. The neighbours were Mr and Mrs Gorsky.

As he leaned down to pick up the ball, young Armstrong heard Mrs Gorsky shouting at Mr Gorsky: 'Sex – you want sex?! You'll get sex when the kid next door walks on the moon!'

True story!

"Gee, Mom, I declare Dad's even more excited about this moonwalk than the kids!"

One weekend four married guys went golfing. During the fourth hole, the following conversation took place.

First guy: 'You have no idea what I had to do to be able to come out golfing this weekend. I had to promise my wife that I will paint every room in the house next weekend.'

Second guy: 'That's nothing. I had to promise my wife that I will build her a new deck for the pool.'

Third guy: 'Man, you both have it easy! I had to promise my wife that I will rebuild the kitchen for her.'

They continued to play the hole, but then they realized that the fourth guy had not said a word. So they asked him, 'You haven't said anything about what you had to do to be able to come golfing this weekend. What's the deal?'

Fourth guy: 'I just set my alarm for 5.30 a.m. When it went off, I shut off my alarm, gave the wife a nudge and said, "Golf course or intercourse?" She said, "Don't forget your sweater."'

The husband should fulfil his marital duty to his wife, and likewise the wife to her husband. The wife's body does not belong to her alone but also to her husband. In the same way, the husband's body does not belong to him alone but also to his wife. Do not deprive each other except by mutual consent and for a time, so that you may devote yourselves to prayer. Then come together again so that Satan will not tempt you because of your lack of self-control.

1 Corinthians 7:3–5, NIV

Bill had always been a prankster. As each of his friends got married, Bill made sure some type of practical joke was played upon them. Now ready to be married himself, he was dreading the payback he knew was coming.

Surprisingly, the ceremony went off without a hitch. No one stood up during the pause to offer a reason 'why this couple should not be married'. His reception wasn't disrupted by streakers or strippers, and the car that the couple were to take on their honeymoon was in perfect working order.

When the couple arrived at their hotel and entered the room, Bill even checked for cornflakes in the bed (a gag he had always loved). Nothing, it seemed, was amiss. Satisfied that they had come away unscathed, the couple fell into bed.

Upon waking, the couple were ravenous, so Bill called down to Room Service and said, 'I'd like to order breakfast for two.'

At that moment, a soft voice from under the bed said, 'Make that five.'

Sex is not the most important part of a love relationship. A Syracuse University survey asked married couples to rank the 10 most important things in a marriage relationship. Caring, a sense of humor and communication came in first, second and third. Sex came in ninth, just ahead of sharing household duties.

Dr Thomas Lickona

Sex is a conversation carried out by other means. If you get on well out of bed, half the problems of bed are solved.

Peter Ustinov

Y

You

It's you I like,
It's not the things you wear.
It's not the way you do your hair,
But it's you I like.
The way you are right now,
The way down deep inside you,
Not the things that hide you.
Not your diplomas...
They're just beside you.
But it's you I like,
Every part of you,
Your skin, your eyes, your feelings,
Whether old or new.
I hope that you'll remember,
Even when you're feeling blue,
That it's you I like,
It's you yourself, it's you,
It's you I like!

Mr Rogers

Zest

Adding zest to your marriage – the top ten tips

The 'marriage-builders' listed below strengthen and add joy and zest to a marriage. Use them liberally with your spouse. Save the list and use it as a check-up to protect the love in your marriage:

- *Listen* to your spouse – always.
- *Value* your spouse's thoughts and interests, even if you don't share them.
- Realize that your spouse is changing and growing as a person daily. *Ask* questions to keep up with the latest.
- *Honour* your spouse when alone, and especially when in front of others.
- Treat your spouse like an *equal* and worthy adult partner.
- *Act* on behalf of your spouse's needs and wishes.
- Use basic *politeness* and courtesy in your marriage.
- Let the natural differences between men and women lead you and your spouse into all sorts of intriguing discussions. *Enjoy* the differences when you can – *accept* them all the other times.
- *Forgive* your spouse.
- *Say* a heartfelt 'I'm sorry' every time you need to.

Rhonda Langefeld

East Dunbartonshire Council